What happens when your worst nightmares come true?
- In a half hour you are meeting your dream date and — uh-oh — your face has just broken out in a ton of zits!
- You've just moved to a new school, and everyone is staring at you — or ignoring you!
- You are supposed to give a presentation in science class next week, and your knees are already knocking!
- All your friends are wearing Guess jeans but your measly baby-sitting job only supports Levi's.
- Your father takes you out to dinner, but the fun stops suddenly when he tells you he's moving out.
- The movie you've been dying to see is finally out and now your little sister wants to tag along with you and your friends!
- The most popular kid in school invites you to a party where you know there will be booze and more.

Overwhelming pressures...every teen's got them. Even Christian teens. But how you deal with them is what's important. *Stressed-Out But Hangin' Tough* offers hints for coping, rather than copping out.

STRESSED-OUT
But Hangin' Tough

Andrea Stephens

Power Books

Fleming H. Revell Company
Old Tappan, New Jersey

Library of Congress Cataloging-in-Publication Data

Stephens, Andrea.
    Stressed-out, but hangin' tough / Andrea Stephens.
      p. cm.
    ISBN 0-8007-5326-7
    1. Stress (Psychology)—Religious   aspects—Christianity—Juvenile literature. 2. Teenagers—Religious life. 3. Teenagers—Conduct of life. I. Title.
BV4531.2.S79 1989
158'.1—dc20   89-10676
                                      CIP

Copyright © 1989 by Andrea Stephens
Published by the Fleming H. Revell Company
Old Tappan, New Jersey 07675
Printed in the United States of America

To my husband, Bill. Thank you for teaching me to take three deep breaths, take time out to relax, and have a little fun when the pressures of life leave me stressed-out!

A Special Thanks To:

Barbra Minar—thanks for previewing and editing this manuscript and adding your expertise on teens and family life.

Carol Lacy—thanks for editing and catching all the technical errors.

Carol Mulker—thanks for typing so quickly . . . sorry I stressed your life with my deadline!

Francie George—thanks for helping me type the rough draft and looking up a zillion Scripture quotes with me.

Jodi Snekvik and **Alan McIntosh**—thanks for being my teen editors . . . your critiques were helpful.

Also, thanks to all the teenagers who completed questionnaires and shared their stress with me. I pray this book will help.

Contents

Preface

Teens today have more opportunities, options, and opinions than ever before. That's great—but it's also stressful. Decisions. Demands. Dilemmas. Disaster.

As you read this book, remember, no matter how stressed you feel or what the cause of your stress is, there is One who can calm your inner storm and set you sailing with renewed strength. His name is Jesus.

Give Jesus your stress, your problems, your worries. In return, He will give you His peace, His strength, and His hope. For He is our ultimate refuge, our hiding place in times of stress. In His presence our stress will decrease for He, Himself, is the Prince of Peace.

> Let him have all your worries and cares, for he is always thinking about you and watching everything that concerns you.
>
> 1 Peter 5:7

PART I

Understanding the Stress Mess

1 This Condition Called Stress

Stressed-out? Stress has become so common it is accepted as a normal part of life. In fact, it's practically fashionable. Stressed-out is the way to be! If you aren't uptight or scrambling around, some people think there must be something wrong with you.

Take a look at Sharon.

It's 7:16 A.M. Sharon was supposed to leave the house by 7:03 A.M. to catch the school bus. But that was the least of her worries. She could stand the embarrassment of being late to first period, but she didn't have her English paper completed. Plus she didn't have her uniform cleaned for gym class and couldn't remember the soccer rules for the quiz. Besides that, she was sure to run into Tom, and she hadn't talked to him since their Saturday night date had ended in a fight. Sharon's mind was racing; her palms were starting to sweat. The knot in her stomach made her feel like throwing up. Her mind screamed, *Why do I feel this way?*

STRESS!

Consider Mark.

It's afternoon now. Mark is home from school. He finished his homework early and doesn't have much else going on. Nothing good on TV. He doesn't want to read. He fidgets around with his younger brother's kickball for a while, then kicks it into the garage. Feeling restless and having nothing else to do, Mark decides to get something to eat. He really can't put his finger on it, but he feels anxious. Why?

STRESS!

Sharon and Mark are both stressed-out! Sharon has too much going on and the pressure is piling up. Mark's stress is different, but it's still stress. He's bored and frustrated. His emotions make him fidgety and anxious.

Exactly what is the condition called stress?

What Is Stress?

Stress is the feeling you get when you experience tension in your life. The tension may be from an overload of demands, as in Sharon's case. It may be from a lack of stimulation and direction, as in Mark's case. Or the tension may be from conflicts you are facing. Tension leads directly to stress.

Think of a rubber band. When you pull a rubber band, it stretches. You are straining it. As you continue to pull, the band gets very tight and tense. You are putting stress on the rubber band! If you stop pulling it, the rubber band relaxes and returns to normal. If you pull as hard as you can what happens? The band breaks!

And that's what you want to avoid!

Some people let stress get to them. Yet, stress doesn't ever have to strain a person to the point of breaking. With God's help you can grow to understand stress, how it affects you, what causes your particular stress, and how you can cope with it. You can get a grip on stress before it gets a grip on you.

I Know I'm Stressed—I Can Feel It

Stress shows itself in your body. It can make you feel or act differently than you normally would. And there's good reason for that.

When you are stressed, a chemical reaction is triggered

in your body. First, your brain sends a direct message to your adrenal glands. Your adrenal glands then flip the switch to release adrenaline and other hormones into your bloodstream.

The adrenaline gets you going—awake, energized, alert, ready for action. Your digestive system shuts down, allowing extra blood to flow to your muscles— they are pumped and ready to go, "Muscles, stand by for instruction." Your heart rate increases and your breathing becomes shallow and short. A light sweat covers your palms. Whether your stress stems from a positive situation or a negative one, you will go through a chemical change. What is important is that you allow yourself to completely recover between each stress reaction, or else you'll be a stress wreck!

If you recover from each stress your stress line will look like this:

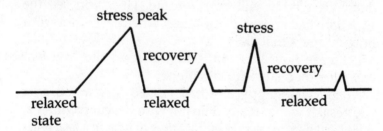

If you never or rarely allow yourself to relax fully again, and you keep letting stresses pile up, your stress line will look like this:

Scary, huh? Looks like the teeth of *Jaws!*

It is possible to learn and apply techniques that will reduce the amount of stress in your life. You can discover how to help yourself fully recover and relax between the stresses. And this book will tell you how!

But first, in case you didn't know. . . .

The Mind-Body Connection

It's true! Your mind and body are connected! And not just physically! What you think in your mind affects what happens in your body. They are inseparable and work together.

If your thoughts are filled with worry and anticipation, your body will be uptight, tense, and you might have a headache, diarrhea, or a twitching foot.

But, if your thoughts are peaceful, calm, and confident, your body will be the same. How you see the situation facing you determines whether or not your brain triggers that chemical reaction.

Let's see how this connection affected the way two teens handled stressful situations.

Kristie was happy she had landed a new job as a waitress. It would really help out with her car payments. But she was worried. *What if I forget to turn in a food order or spill an entire milkshake in someone's lap? And what if the restaurant is packed? Can I serve all those tables at once?* She just wasn't sure of herself. She felt a headache coming on, and she didn't even have to report to work for two more hours!

Kristie let all the things that could possibly go wrong fill her thoughts and she became stressed. And she had two whole hours of worry until it would be time to start work. She perceived her new job in a way that resulted in a headache and nervous body.

Jeff was going to be playing quarterback in the final

game of the season. He knew that the outcome of the game and the team's chance to go to the regional finals depended greatly on his performance. He went over the plays in his mind and told himself he would do his best and that was all anyone could expect. Jeff played very well, and the team won.

Jeff had the right to get nervous and stressed-out. But he didn't. He could have imagined his situation as extremely frightful. What if he goofed up? The team was counting on him. Getting uptight just would have made Jeff's muscles tense and increased his chances of fumbling. Staying calm kept his coordination intact. He maintained an accurate perception of the game and all went well.

The way you see your situation and the thoughts you have about it will affect how stressed-out you get. Some of your stress reactions will be mild; others will be major. Exactly how will you know how you are stressed? What symptoms will you have? What signals should you look for? Read on.

2 Sneaky Symptoms of Stress

Stress pops its head up in many different ways. Its symptoms may be physical or emotional.

Physical Symptoms: Help! My Body Is Falling Apart

These physical symptoms are your body's way of telling you something is wrong. "Wake up," it says. Something is out of whack or being neglected. Though it may take your brain a while to catch on, your body consistently sends you messages.

Not everyone reacts to stress in the same way. Especially physically. Stress seems to be able to find the weakest part of our physical makeup and take up residence there. For example, many people have weak lower backs. Every time they get stressed, that same spot in their back starts acting up. The same could be true for headaches, sinuses, joints, and so on.

Doesn't it figure that one of the most common physical symptoms of stress is one that appears over and over ... ZITS! Blemishes. Facial break-out. Whatever you want to call them, they proudly display themselves where the whole world can see, thank you very much. But, at least they are not life-threatening and can be easily cured and covered up, whereas many other symptoms cannot.

As you read over this list of physical symptoms, keep in mind that the more severe symptoms included are from prolonged stress. Rarely does someone have a heart attack just from the stress of a math test or a first date! Here they are:

blemishes	viruses or infections
skin disorders and rashes	sinus problems
aching muscles or spasms	frequent colds or flu
frequent headaches	tightness in jaw
racing heart	hair loss
tiredness	increase or decrease in appetite
diarrhea	cold hands or feet
dry mouth	temporary loss of menstruation
nausea or nervous stomach	high blood pressure
shortness of breath	ulcers
sweaty palms and underarms	heart attack

The list of physical symptoms can seem so overwhelming that you would think you could blame every little ache and pain in your life on stress. Listen to your body and you will find out how a situation is affecting you. Your symptoms will tell the truth.

Emotional Symptoms: Help! I Can't Stand the Way I Feel

Often when people are stressed-out, their emotions are thrown out of line. It may cause them to be more tearful or perhaps act more rebellious than they normally would. Can you guess who gets more tearful and who gets more rebellious? Guys or girls? Typically, girls cry and guys want to fight, but that can be switched around!

Stress is strange. It can cause you to get upset by things that usually don't bother you. And with the things that normally do bug you—watch out!

Emotional stress is often the culprit behind our out-of-the-ordinary actions. People who are usually outgoing may withdraw and start acting shy. They may prefer staying home to going out with friends, and they lose interest in the things they normally enjoy.

Then there are those usually quiet ones who get loud, brash, and extra talkative; suddenly they're the class clown or loudmouth. Emotions and behavior are closely linked.

Here are some of the many emotional symptoms usually felt under stress:

fear	irritability
worry	guilt
fatigue	anger
depression	resentment
mood swings	boredom
anxiety	impatience
dissatisfaction	hopelessness
discontentment	uselessness

Do any of these ring a bell with you? Maybe you have noticed some of these symptoms in your friends or family members. Thank heaven all of these symptoms don't strike at the same time. In fact, we generally experience just one or two symptoms at once. But that is enough to wake us up to our own stress. By paying attention, we realize that we need to make some changes. Then we change what we can and learn to accept what we can't change.

Evidence that you are stressed-out is easy for most people to see—thanks to the symptoms you show. Signs of stress show up in your behavior, your spiritual life, and your unconscious habits.

Basic Behavioral Signs: "Honest, the Stress Made Me Do It"

The behaviors listed here are common and predictable reactions to stress. This list could be miles long because we all react differently to stress. These, however, are the most frequent teenage reactions to stress. Can you relate to some of them?

Unable to sleep
Craving sleep
Can't sit still
Having a hard time making decisions
Pulling away from others
Acting childishly
Being overly loud
Laughing at inappropriate times, or uncontrollably
Crying
Rebelling
Overeating
Not wanting to eat
Being short-tempered
Can't get organized
Not finishing things you start

Stressed-out behaviors can greatly affect the way you perform. Whether it's your lack of concentration during class that shows up at test time or being late for work because you're crying hysterically over your boyfriend, performance gets messed up!

Let's take a look at some teens trying to perform while stressed-out.

Gary wasn't reacting very well to the news. His brain was completely crowded with the worst possible thoughts. *Are the other kids at school going to make fun of me? Will I ever live this one down?* Gary's teachers and parents had decided—Gary was to be held back a year in school. All of his friends would go on to high school. Not Gary. His tangled thoughts were making it even harder to pay attention during class. Great. That, of course, made the situation worse because he was getting even further behind at school.

Karen had just taken on too many responsibilities and was feeling swallowed up by all the demands on her. She kept a daily appointment book, but even so, she was having a hard time getting organized. There was just too much to do. And now she was starting to forget important things—her brother's birthday, her Spanish quiz, where she put her checkbook. Was she losing her mind?

Ann was having a hard time at home. Her parents fought constantly, and they rarely talked to her unless, of course, there was something they wanted her to do. She felt alone and isolated. She felt that everything happening around her was out of her control. She was stressed. Ann expressed her need to have control by refusing to eat. At least, that was one thing she *could* be in charge of. It was also her quiet way of rebelling against her parents. Ann was showing signs of anorexia.

Andy held several track records at his high school. He was good in many events, especially high hurdles. But today's meet didn't go so well. Andy's grandfather is in the hospital recovering from a major heart attack. Andy was thinking about all the times his grandfather had taken him fishing and quail hunting. Plus he always came to Andy's track meets. But not today. Andy approached the hurdles as usual but accidentally hit the tops of two hurdles, sending them to the ground. He could hardly believe it.

Gary's stress over being held back a grade was making it nearly impossible for him to concentrate at school. That, as we mentioned, was only making his situation worse.

Karen's overloaded schedule left her feeling disorganized. And those momentary memory lapses made her feel so dumb.

The stress Ann felt over her homelife had greatly disrupted her eating patterns. Her loss of appetite and desire to have control are leading her down the road to a head-on collision with anorexia nervosa.

Andy's worry over his grandfather's heart attack was affecting his physical coordination. His track events turned out miserably.

The stressful situation in each teen's life was affecting his or her performance. Stress seems to trigger a chain reaction. First you have the stressful situation. That leads to the symptoms, either physical or emotional. Next your behavior is affected. Last, your performance is disrupted.

Stressful situation → symptom → behavior → performance. The first leads to the next and the next and the next! Often you can discover the cause of your stress by tracing these reactions backwards. Just try it in the reverse order. First recognize the breakdown in your performance. This helps you identify your behavior, which helps you uncover the symptoms, which finally point to the cause. Give it a try.

Spiritual Signs: "Dear God, Are You Really There?"

When you are feeling the symptoms of stress and the challenge of daily living is getting the best of you, your spiritual life can suffer.

You might even find yourself asking:

"God, why are You letting this happen to me? Don't You know I can't handle this alone? Where are You?"

The desire to pray, attend church or youth group, or read the Bible is out the window. In fact, you might even feel indifferent toward God and start letting doubts creep in. Stress can quench your motivation and your faith.

We often end up running away from God rather than to Him. Running away from God accomplishes nothing. Well, at least it doesn't do anything to solve your problems. You are only delaying your troubles by unplugging yourself from the one Source that can calm your fears and guide you through every stress storm in life. You will find the strength, comfort, and direction that you need when you dive toward God, not drop away from Him.

If you feel God has rejected you or abandoned you, forcing you to "go it alone" through the tough times of life, you are wrong. He has promised in His Word not to ever leave us or forsake us. If God seems far away, stop and ask yourself, "Has God moved away or have I?"

James 4:8 assures us that when we draw near to God, He will draw near to us. Perhaps without really realizing, you have been avoiding God. Now you find yourself trailing behind in the relationship you used to have with Him. Or maybe you've just never gotten close to God.

When times seem hard and stress is plaguing your life, you need the insight God can give. Go ahead; talk to Him in prayer. Read a little bit of the Bible. Just run to the Lord. He understands and can help. He is waiting for you with open arms!

Balance Is Best

Prolonged stress slowly chisels away at the body's immune system, making its defenses weak. This causes the body to be more susceptible to infection, viruses, and illness. In fact, it is said that the majority of today's illnesses are caused by stress.

This has been true for several teenagers I know.

When Lonnie gets uptight over school—just school in general, which, as you know, lasts nine months out of the year—she catches a cold that seems to last forever. She tries to shake it, but the cold persists. Whether she realizes it or not, her stress has gotten her immune system down. Until Lonnie deals with her dislike of school, she probably won't get well—except during the school-free summer months!

Craig's stress-caused illness is different but valid. His dad was diagnosed with cancer two and a half years ago and is slowly getting worse. Being the oldest son, Craig has taken a full-time job, working after swim team practice until midnight and on the weekends. He is helping the family make ends meet, participating in a sport, and trying to maintain his 3.6 GPA so that he can get into a good college. But he is not doing all of this without stress. Craig has a spot on the lower back of his head where he keeps losing his hair. The stress he is under is really getting to him.

Positive Situation Stress

Stress caused by a positive situation in your life is called *eustress*. This stress is from situations that are good, but still stressful, like your first date, performing in the school play, a new family member, or holiday gatherings. It's the kind of stress that puts you on the cutting edge. Maybe it helps you perform better. You might even find this kind of stress pleasurable. It's fun—like being excited. Yet, your body still responds, because to your body, stress is stress!

Imagine yourself in this situation:

Your school science project has been entered in a state science competition. You are about to make a presentation of your project in front of the other chosen students and a panel of five judges. You have confidence in your project and you feel really excited. Those ol' butterflies are acting up and they have your stomach in knots. You are finding it harder to breathe. In fact, your breathing has gotten shallow and very short. There go your palms—sweat, sweat, sweat. Yet, you feel up, and your thinking is clear and alert. Okay, it's almost your turn. The guy ahead of you made a great presentation. You're on! Your hands shake as you approach the microphone. You are alert and ready, GO . . . Ah. Great delivery. Better than you expected. Now you can relax.

Did you get a little uncomfortable just reading this? Maybe so. What happened in this illustration is the pressure you were under supplied you with the extra boost of adrenaline and blood flow you needed to make you alert, attentive, and sharp for your presentation. When it was over, it was over. Your body let down; you relaxed. The situation was positive—you were being honored for your science project. Still, this situation produced stress.

Negative Situation Stress

Now think about this situation:

You are caught cheating on an algebra test along with a group of your friends. You had forgotten about the test and didn't study ahead of time. It all seemed innocent enough. But your excuses aren't going to help you now. One by one, each of you is being marched down to the principal's office and your parents are being called. Ultimate embarrassment for you and your parents. How are you going to explain this one? And your dad was just elected to the school board! You're waiting your turn. Your body's so tense that your lower back and legs are aching. And even though it's lunch break, you couldn't eat if it was the last meal you'd ever have. Okay, it's your turn to face the principal and your parents.

If you have ever been called to the principal's office, you can probably relate to this story. Yes, you made the wrong decision, cheated on your test, and got caught.

Your body goes into instant stress convulsions. This kind of stress is caused by a negative situation and is called *distress*.

You can eliminate some of the stress-producing things in your life but not all of them (nagging little brothers or sisters, school, just to name a few). Nor should you eliminate everything. You will benefit most by figuring out what your stress symptoms are and learning to handle the stresses you face.

3 Personal Stress Inventory

It's time for your personal stress inventory! Have you recognized glimpses of yourself in the first two chapters? Are you starting to understand how important it is to know how you respond to stress?

Take a few minutes to take this stress checkup and see how you check out. Please refer to the lists of stress symptoms, signs, and behaviors, from the previous chapters.

First of all, how would you describe stress?

When you are feeling particularly worried about something, what are your physical symptoms? In other words, where and what are your aches and pains?

Emotions can run high or low when stress is on your doorstep. List the emotions you experience with your stress.

What is your outlook on life when you feel stressed? For instance: discouraged, hopeful, challenged, etc.

In what ways does your behavior change when you are stressed?

How is your performance interrupted or improved during stress?

Do you tend to draw near to the Lord or away from Him during stress? How does your spiritual life change?

What positive situation has recently caused you to experience positive stress or *eustress?*

What unpleasant situation has recently caused you to experience negative stress or *distress?*

Are you becoming aware of your reactions to stress? Great! Do you see room for some stress reduction?

Personality and Your Stress Responses

What pushes your stress buttons and gets your motor going may not even faze your best friend or your sister. You may have thought, *What's wrong with me? Why do I get strung out when nobody else does? I must be weird.* Or for that matter you may have thought someone else is over-sensitive for flipping out over what to you seems to be no big deal. Relax! You're not weird and they are not over-sensitive. We just don't all get revved up over the same things.

Your personality has a lot to do with the way you react

to stress. Some personalities get more stressed. Some get less stressed. Our anger level, patience level, hormone balance, sense of humor, vulnerability—all of these and more make up our individual personalities.

In fact, because of all the different personality types in the world there will be many different reactions—even to the same situation.

Let's imagine a situation.

Four students just got sentenced to detention for not having an assignment finished on time. None of these students had ever been detained before. Here's how they reacted:

Kevin couldn't have cared less. Sure, he worked on the assignment but just didn't finish. No biggie. Detention wouldn't be so bad. It would just make him late for meeting the guys at Video World.

Stress Level: On a scale of 1 to 10, Kevin gets a 1.

Marie burst into tears. Detention? How could she face her friends? And what about her parents? They would be so embarrassed. She had always been an *A* student. One little late assignment and she gets total doom for it. Marie didn't intend to hand the assignment in late. It just happened.

Stress Level: Marie's stress scores a 7.

Lindee smirked. She was sort of excited but didn't want to show it. She meant to work on her assignment but there was this party she couldn't miss. It was hosted by the best-looking guy at school and *she* was invited. Detention would be a kick. Most of the guys from the party ended up in detention almost every day. It would just be a social hour for her. Who knows, maybe she could get a date out of it.

Stress Level: Lindee places about a 4 on the stress scale.

Todd was furious. "How dare he send me to detention. He really has a lot of nerve," Todd spouted to his friends. Todd thought detention was uncalled for. After class he was going straight to the principal's office. Nobody was going to punish him and get away with it.

Stress Level: Todd gets a 10.

Four different personalities, four different ways to react, and yet the same situation.

Do you see how we are not all stressed by the same situations? And that's okay! What stresses you out is neither right nor wrong. It's part of you. The way you see the situation causes your reaction to it. And the way you see it is influenced by your personality.

Isn't it great how God made us so unique? No two people are alike. We each look different, act differently, respond differently, and have our own unique personalities.

Psalm 139:1–4 tells us the Lord knows our thoughts, our actions, and our words even before we say them. He knows us intimately and He understands us. And—the good news—He still loves us! What a big God we have!

He is also concerned about us. He cares that we get stressed and sometimes feel like we can't handle all that life throws at us. He wants us to learn to handle our stress. But before we learn to cope, we need to identify the cause!

PART II
Here's the Rough Stuff

4 The Big Ten

Now we're getting to the good stuff—the causes of teenage stress! So far we have been very loose with the term *stress*. We defined it as the demands or pressures that we experience. Some are pressures we put on ourselves; some are pressures put on us by others or life itself! Yet, what exactly are these demands and pressures that make teens feel strung out?

To answer this question, I surveyed over a hundred teens, both girls and guys. From their intense, honest, and open answers comes this list of the ten most common causes of teenage stress.

"Are there really only ten?" you ask.

No!

The causes of stress are innumerable. As we already learned, what leaves one person anxious may leave someone else feeling calm, cool, and collected. We are not all stressed by the same things. Therefore, it is impossible to list here all the causes of stress. So, what you are about to read are the top ten most-reported causes of teenage stress.

School
Family
Friends
Dating
Popularity
Self-image
Money
Future
Fast-paced life-style
Christianity

In the next ten chapters you will see exactly what it is about each of these topics that causes all the tension, upset, worry, headaches, stomachaches, and so on, teens go through.

Perhaps this information will help you get in touch with exactly what stresses you personally in each of these areas. For instance, you may already know that life with your parents is a real pressure cooker. But can you pinpoint what it is about your relationship with your parents that causes the stress? Perhaps it is their expectations about your life—getting *A*'s, doing chores, getting a job, or being popular. Or maybe it is their personalities or inconsistencies that get on your nerves.

When you can identify the root cause of your stress, you can begin to deal with it effectively. Sometimes, just knowing what's bothering you eases some of the pressure.

At the end of each chapter there is a special page to "Express Yourself." This is where you can write down your personal stresses in each area that we've discussed. It is possible that you may be stressed-out by something not even mentioned in that chapter. Great! Write it down. Get in touch with yourself!

On the bottom half of the Express Yourself page, you will find stress-relieving Scriptures that deal specifically with the topic of that chapter. Don't cheat yourself. Take the time to read each of these Scriptures to see what helpful hints God's Word offers on the ten top causes of teenage stress.

5 School: The Number One Stress!

I had just met Cindy that night. It was her first visit to youth group and her experience at school was making her feel nervous about it.

Cindy was new at the high school and was finding it hard to adjust. "There are so many cliques. I can't believe it! When I walk down the halls, everyone just looks at me. No one smiles, no one says 'Hello.' Plus, the classes are hard. I hate it."

The tension in Cindy's voice and the tears welling up in her eyes told me that Cindy was stressed. It's tough to make new friends; it's tough breaking in and finding your place; it's tough getting used to a new curriculum; it's just plain tough.

School ranked as the number one stress among the students I interviewed. That's not surprising since school fills thousands of hours of a teen's life each year.

What exactly is stressful about school?

Everything, was the resounding answer! But here are some specifics.

Grades

Take grades for starters.

Striving for high grades is honorable and the payoff is

worthwhile. But with it comes lots of pressure and competition. Teachers and parents are on your back to study, try harder, push yourself, succeed.

Many kids want to please their parents and get high scores. But when they don't, they feel like failures. Worse yet, they feel dumb. It's especially hurtful when they have a brother or sister who breezes through with A's every time.

"I get tired of competing and trying to please everyone—especially my parents. I end up feeling like I've really blown it. But I tried my best," says Kim.

School just comes easier for some people and many kids need to ease up on their own self-demands. Not that they should quit trying, but they should quit feeling so guilty for not getting straight A's.

Academics can be extra hard for teens who are creative, not studious. That was the case with Sue. Her parents required that she take honors courses in English, Geometry, Physics, and German all in the same semester. She knew she would struggle and she did—C's and D's. Doing poorly was killing her self-image and causing a lot of fighting at home.

Sue was restless when she tried to study. But when she took a study break and went to the piano she found relief. She loved to play the piano and it was easy for her. So was art; Sue could spend hours working on her watercolor paintings. Her parents wanted her to take academic subjects at school, not music and art. Yet, their requirements weren't working. After months of struggle, Sue got her school guidance counselor to convince her parents to let her adjust her class schedule for the next semester.

They finally agreed.

The results? Three A's, one B, and only one C. Soon Sue's outlook on school changed. Her parents eased up because they were so pleased with her new grades, and Sue was feeling better about herself.

Some creative personalities may have a hard time with academic subjects and vice versa. It's important that everyone get a well-balanced education, but it's equally important to know your abilities and talents. It can make your school years much better.

Homework

Sometimes you think it will never end. And why does every teacher believe in giving homework every night? Do they get together to plan this?

"At my school," says Tim, "we don't have any free periods. They don't believe in study hall, so that leaves all of my homework for after school."

This is a particular hardship on kids who are involved in extracurricular activities like drama, debate, student government, the school newspaper, clubs, or sports. Keeping up with homework is a major cause of stress. It means constant study after school, in the evening, or in the morning before school. If you take a break, even for one night, you run the risk of falling behind.

No doubt about it, homework can give you a headache!

Tests

Many sleepless nights have been caused by the worry over tests. Perhaps you missed some classes or are behind in your reading. Just facing a test makes you sweat.

And what happens when you have several tests on the same day?

Major stress.

Test taking is tough. One student shared that she gets hyper and breaks down in tears before test day. She found, however, that her stress was relieved if she disciplined herself and spent more time studying (there goes TV time). If she wrote up a sample test for herself, she did better on her tests. They weren't so scary when she was more prepared. Teens reported that having homework, tests, speeches to give, and projects due all at the same time was another big stress. Many kids want to give up, but they realize that doesn't get them anywhere!

Extracurricular Activities

Schools today offer so many opportunities. But they also give you a chance to spread yourself so thin you'll end up a stress mess. Choosing which activities to be involved in may be tough. You need to prioritize so that you participate in the things you can get the most out of or those you enjoy the most. If you try to do it all, watch out!

My friend Mary is fifteen ("soon to be sixteen," she always reminds me), a good student, a Christian, a leader on campus, and a cheerleader.

Student council meetings before school three mornings a week, cheerleading practice, football games to cheer, youth group, church choir, voice lessons, dance class, yearbook meetings, pep club, student Bible club, teacher's assistant—just hearing about Mary's schedule exhausts me! And when she was on the swim team, life was even more hectic.

What concerns me (and Mary's mother) is that Mary gets so tired. She feels overwhelmed trying to keep up. She begins and ends many days in tears. Colds, sore throats, earaches, and headaches are everyday occurrences for Mary.

Some teens try to do it all. But they pay a precious price for it. Mary would benefit by eliminating one or two of her activities from her schedule. She would be a healthier and happier young lady.

How about you?

Enjoy extracurricular activities. Don't make them a chore!

Competition

"What I can't stand is getting back papers in class and all the smart kids start showing off their grades to each other," remarked sixteen-year-old Jim. "Then they have the nerve to ask, 'What did you get?' to everyone around them—including me. No way am I showing my grade. Sometimes I make up a higher grade, just to make them wonder. I get tired of everyone trying to impress everyone else."

School is a great breeding ground for competition with all the comparing going on. But comparing leaves you feeling that you aren't good enough or that you're better than others, and both these attitudes can be dangerous.

You are your own competition. Whether you're competing for grades, sports, or drama, challenge yourself to improve your personal performance or just to maintain where you are. Forget about the other kids and be your best self!

Other School Stresses

Many other causes of stress at school were reported.

Being called on in class. This one rated high. Some teens are too shy to talk in front of a class; others aren't sure of the answer. The dead silence while the teacher waits can be dreadful.

Changing schools. Whether it's transferring to a new school or moving up from junior high to high school, changing schools can cause some serious sweating! Of course, this involves making new friends. This is one of the most self-conscious times of any teenager's life!

Meaningful subjects. Teens through the years have been baffled over this one—why study subjects that you will never use later in your life? Algebra, geometry, physics, ancient history.

Flunking out. Need I say more?

Being held back a year. This can be embarrassing, but better for you in the long run—though it can make you want to hibernate the entire summer and reappear on the school scene in disguise!

Giving speeches. Being up in front of the class or speaking in front of any group, for that matter, gets your knees knocking and your palms sweating.

Enduring suspension and detention. You can just feel the stress, can't you?

Teachers. Some teachers are great. They are encouraging, supportive, and understanding. But others—forget it! Kids reported that some teachers swear at them in class, throw objects at them, and punish them just because they feel like it. Not to say that every teen who has ever been sent to the principal's office was totally innocent.

Rules. So many rules. Do this! Don't do that! Can't walk in the halls between classes without a pass. Can't use the telephone without permission. Can't leave campus at lunchtime. On and on. School can seem like a prison to teens. But most rules are made for a decent and respectable reason—to protect you and keep order. Try to see them from the administration's point of view.

Even though school ranked as the number one stress, school is valuable! It's necessary to learn in order to live in this world. Yet, no matter how you look at it, school produces stress. Some of the situations cause good stress. Some cause distress. Learning to deal with these stresses will help you cope with school.

Express Yourself

What are your school-related stresses? Grades, homework, tests, extracurricular activities, teachers, giving speeches, others? Record your stresses here. Remember, identifying your stress is the first step in dealing with it.

Your personal school stresses:

Stress-Relieving Scriptures

Proverbs 23:12 (NAS) — Apply your heart to discipline, and your ears to words of knowledge.

Proverbs 3:21, 22 — Have two goals: wisdom—that is, knowing and doing right—and common sense. Don't let them slip away, for they fill you with living energy, and are a feather in your cap.

Proverbs 1:7 — How does a man become wise? The first step is to trust and reverence the Lord! Only fools refuse to be taught.

2 Timothy 2:15 (KJV) — Study to shew thyself approved unto God. . . .

6 The Family Portrait

Have you ever had your family picture taken?

It's a scream, isn't it? All the family members take showers—even rebel Randy—then, put on their Sunday clothes, comb their hair, brush their teeth, pile into the station wagon, and head down to the photo studio.

Halfway there, the right front tire blows, and while changing it Dad gets grease on his suit jacket. The baby spits up on Mom's new dress. Little Jimmy and Jamie are pulling each other's hair and screaming their heads off. Randy is sitting in the back of the wagon with his headphones on, swaying back and forth completely oblivious!

Finally, they arrive. "Next, please. Oh, what a charming family," the photo assistant says with a plastered smile. Okay, everyone's seated, squashed together, smiling, saying "Cheese." Great! It's over.

Two weeks later the proofs come in. Oh, aren't they sweet. What a special family.

Stress-free, right?

Family portraits don't always give you the real picture. They don't tell you that Mom and Dad have been bickering, that older sister is crushed from a broken romance, that little brother's foot is bruised from being run over by a motorbike, that . . . well, you know. Family life is not stress-free. Yet, the family was God's idea. Even Jesus was born into a family. He understands what family life is like and He can help us with ours! Let's see what our questionnaires had to say about family life. Parents first!

Problems With Parents

As a small child, your parents are your providers, your protectors, your playmates. By the time you edge your

46

way into the teenage years, you may feel your parents are from the Stone Age or are runaway aliens! You can't seem to figure them out or relate to them. Everything they do, say, and wear embarrasses you. By the time you reach young adulthood, however, you begin to see the wisdom, the love, the genuine concern in your parents. And though you never thought it was possible, you become friends with them.

This journey you take through life with your parents goes through many changes. As a teen, where are you now in the journey?

Aliens, right? You're sure your parents are from another planet!

Expectant Expectations

Nicole was struggling with her parents. They wanted her to do well in school, attend youth group and Sunday school, and do her share of chores around the house. They also wanted her to be active at school and be popular. And when she didn't have a date for the Homecoming Dance, they worried.

Expectations. Some of them are so hard to live up to. Especially when they are your *parents'* expectations for you. Naturally, deep down most teens want to please their parents. It's just that they think they can't, so they figure, "Why bother trying?" Trying to please some parents can leave you feeling exhausted. Have you ever been frustrated by this?

Parents' expectations vary. Most parents expect their kids to try their best in school—some even pressure them to get high grades. Or perhaps they push for their child to always do the right thing at the right time in the right way—perfection!

Uh-oh, major problem. No one is perfect!

Parents put pressure on you for several reasons. One

is they want you to do your best so you can succeed in life. They want you to be able to survive out there in that big old world, so they push for you to excel and to be prepared for whatever might face you.

Parents may start insisting that you get a job and start paying for the extras that you want. That's because they know that after you graduate and get out on your own, you can't survive with an empty wallet. You may get ticked and think they are being unfair, but they want you to be responsible for yourself in the future. They know from experience that no one is going to give you money, including them.

Another right reason parents put pressure on their kids is that they want them to take advantage of the opportunities which they, as young people, never had.

Many parents make major sacrifices to provide extra opportunities for their kids. Mom forgoes a new Sunday dress so Susan can have another few months of piano lessons. Dad keeps repairing the old lawn mower to provide the extra cash for Toby's football camp tuition. And how many teens take these things for granted?

But, let's face it, parents are not perfect.

Sometimes parents put pressure on their kids for the wrong reasons, reasons that can hurt kids' feelings or make them feel resentful.

Some parents want their teens to make *them* look good. When the child does well, it reflects on the parents' ability to raise kids. Plus, parents derive attention from their children's successes. Parents don't want their kids to be social embarrassments to them. This is totally natural and understandable—parents are human—but it can be unfair to the kids!

Some parents want their teens to be popular because it makes them feel popular. So, they pour on the pressure—be smart, be cute, be funny, be social, be part of all the activities, be wholesome, be like so-and-so. Yes, sad as it may seem, parents can have a problem accepting their own kids for who they are, loving them just because they are their own flesh and blood, a gift from God. Please note that I have said *some* parents have wrong reasons for putting pressure on their kids. Your parents may not.

Please Love Me

This leads us to another major cause of stress between parents and their teens: the need to feel loved. Calvin said, "When my parents nag me all the time it makes it hard to believe that they love me." Kids often misinterpret pressure from their parents as a sign of disapproval. They think their parents don't love them. Everyone needs to feel loved. Some teens choose to go elsewhere for that love when they are not getting it at home.

Please listen to this:

If you do not feel loved at home and feel as if you can't talk it over with your parents, then build up a network of good, close friends from whom you can get the love you need. Maybe you feel that your grandparents or relatives love you more than your parents. Great! Spend more time with them. Or get a pet. Dogs and cats have a way of making us feel loved when no one else can.

But don't—I repeat—*don't* run to the arms of an available girl or guy and get involved in a serious, dependent or sexual relationship. Yes, there can be temporary feelings of love and acceptance from that person, but when the relationship breaks up, there you are, alone again and feeling unloved. Almost all teenage romances break up. Very few end up in marriage. And if you get so involved that you say yes to having sexual experiences with that person, you will only be more torn up later. It's better to put your time and effort into developing a few close friends of the same sex.

Feeling unloved is often the result of separation and divorce. Missy wrote, "One of my major stresses is not seeing my dad. He lives in another state and I never get to see him. My parents act like they really hate each other. I hope that when they see me I am a reminder of the love they used to share, not a reminder of the hate they now feel. I only want them to love me."

With so much divorce in our world, Missy is not the only one who feels this way. It's helpful for kids to remember that their parents are hurting and struggling through the divorce themselves. It's painful for everyone involved. Yet, it doesn't mean parents love their kids any less. It may be difficult for parents to show that love while they are hurting, but the love is still there.

Tim writes, "When I don't feel loved, I usually end up feeling lonely." Believe me, everyone, at some time in his or her life, struggles with feeling unloved, unlovable, or lonely. Loneliness is a major problem. Your tattered old teddy bear from days gone by can't wrap his furry little arms around you when you cry in bed at night.

If love is not coming from your parents, please let me assure you of this: You have a heavenly Father who adores you. No love for you can ever be greater than His. If you develop a love relationship with God, it will be one that lasts forever. Whether other people come and go in your life won't matter quite so much. The Lord's love is forever and unchanging. You can count on it!

Divorce: The Family Killer

A large percentage of the teens I interviewed were from divorced, separated, or troubled homes. They were stressed from the fighting, the loud voices, the tears, the slamming doors, the silent treatment, and the fear of never seeing one of their parents again. They were also dealing with anger at their parents for not trying hard enough to make the marriage work. Now they were labeled teenagers from broken homes—something over which they had no control.

This was the situation in Scott's case. He was in shock. He knew his parents were having problems, but he never thought it would go this far. One afternoon he came home from school and found his dad crying. His mom had moved out. Had they thought about him? He wondered how this would make him feel and look? He had always bragged about having both his parents at home. Not anymore.

The image of the happy, whole family that kids need is broken when parents divorce. The whole world suddenly knows that life at home has been rough and they have failed. Most teens said that they felt embarrassed, hurt, and angry when their parents broke up.

When divorce strikes, a whole new set of stresses stares teens in the face. Who will I live with? Will I have to go to court? Will my parents ever talk again? Will we all have to get jobs so we have enough money to live? What will my friends say? Will people think there is something wrong with me? Will God be mad at my parents? At me? On and on.

Yet, for some, the tensions of homelife may be lessened by the divorce. Marcy found that even though her dad was not at home anymore—and that bothered her—the house was more peaceful. She was glad she didn't have to listen to arguing twenty hours a day.

Living in a single-parent family was reported as another major stress. Whether living with Mom or Dad, new ground rules are laid out, things change. Most common is the worry over finances. The parent who is gone may or may not pay child support, leaving the family to fend for themselves. Mom, who wasn't working, must now find a job. At this time, the remaining family will benefit from pulling together, being supportive and understanding of each other, and helping out.

Ken was maintaining his good grades, his office as vice-president of the student body, and his goalie position on the soccer team fairly well. But when his parents split, things were different. His mom didn't make enough to pay for any extras. In fact, just covering the rent, utilities, and food was a struggle. Ken knew he had to help out. One of his activities would have to go so he could get a job. He decided to drop soccer. After all, just trying to pay for the shoes and uniform was an expense in itself. He didn't feel super-resentful because he was still able to be involved with student government and keep his grades up, which was important for his future goal—law school.

Laura's family found the money crunch harder to handle. Even though she was baby-sitting as often as she could, it was barely enough to buy her an occasional new outfit for school. She felt cheated. Sometimes she would save up her lunch money to go to the movies with her friends on Saturday night. But getting enough to go on the class trip, get a permanent, take dance lessons, go to a concert, or get new track shoes—no way. And where would be the excitement of getting her driver's license? There was no car for her to drive. Life didn't seem fair to Laura.

Well, life isn't always fair.

We don't ask for the situations we often find ourselves in. Yet, God will make our situations work out for good because we love Him. Turn to God with a sense of optimism, not resentment. Get psyched about the good things He's going to do!

Having parents who are dating is another stress associated with divorce and living with a single parent.

Take Gina.

She acted so flippant when she told me this story, but

I knew she was hurting. Her mom had been divorced for over a year. She met a man at work, someone she sort of liked. When he asked Gina's mom out for dinner, she said yes. She made such a big deal out of her "first date," Gina wanted to gag.

"What should I wear? My blue dress or this cream pantsuit?" Gina's mom asked excitedly. Gina said that she didn't care what her mom wore. She went on to imitate her mom fussing with her hair, getting her lipstick on just right, carefully selecting a fragrance for the evening, then calling up one of her friends to engage in girlish chatter over the whole ordeal. Then, Gina's mother came home from her date at 2:00 A.M. Gina was beside herself with rage and jealousy.

Gina wasn't allowed to stay out late. In fact the whole situation was flip-flopped from the norm. Gina felt like the mother watching her teenage daughter get ready for her first date, then getting upset when she broke the rules and stayed out too late. All of this was a particularly sore spot for Gina because she didn't do much dating.

Watching your parents date is rough. It's not something most kids think about when they're growing up. They want Mom and Dad to love each other. For some teens, this part of it is too much to swallow, so they ignore it, deny it, act like it is no big deal. Here they are trying to figure out their own sexual identity when suddenly their parents are doing the same thing. They have never thought of their parents as sexual beings. To see parents flirt, act affectionate to someone other than their original spouse, is too hard for many teens to accept. Not all situations are the same. Hopefully, most dating parents use more wisdom than Gina's mom did.

Other Parent Stresses

My parents don't trust me. This is a common complaint among teens. Why their parents don't trust them is a question they must answer themselves. Maybe they've given their parents reason not to trust them. But trust *can* be regained. Go where you say you are going, do what you tell your parents you are going to do, spend the money they give you on what it was designated for, come home at the time they have set.

Rules and regulations. Many teens reported that the "laws of the house" were something they didn't like and usually didn't agree with. Try to discuss household regulations with your parents. See if you can reach some compromises, then abide by them. Life at home will be much smoother. Understand that your parents have been commissioned by God to raise you, watch over you, protect you, provide for you, and discipline you. I know some parents overdo it, but your cooperative attitude will lessen the stress.

Accepting parents. Teens struggle with the guilt of not liking their parents' personalities and not wanting them around so much. This is especially true when teens are forming their own identities and trying to achieve their independence. Accept your parents for who and what they are.

Accepting stepparents. Though teens can have a good relationship with their stepparents, many do not. One young man said the biggest stress in his life was his stepdad. Kids might find themselves having a hard time respecting a stepparent as a true parent. This is especially true if you gain a stepparent in your teen years.

Being with parents. Though some teens want to stay away from their parents, many want to be with them. Several teens reported feeling guilty about not spending more time at home or doing things with their parents.

Feeling misunderstood. Several kids reported that their parents do not understand them. Communication can be a real problem in families. Talking is very vital to good parent-child relationships.

Arguing. Heated discussions and arguing do not happen only in troubled homes, but also in normal, healthy homes. Healthy homes, however, have learned to forgive, let go, and keep loving.

Setting an example. Do as I say, not as I do! Many teens get stressed over their parents' inconsistency. They think their parents are hypocrites. We all have imperfections and inconsistencies. It gives us areas to work on. Be forgiving toward others, especially your parents!

Sibling Stress: Brothers and Sisters

Family relationships and stresses are not limited to your parents. In fact, you may get along great with your parents, but your sister or brother drives you crazy!

The major causes of stress between siblings—sisters and sisters, brothers and brothers, and sisters and brothers—were reported to be these:

Being jealous.
Sharing a bedroom. One may be sloppy, one may be neat.
Sharing the bathroom. Oh, boy!
Being teased or ganged up on.
Competing with each other, whether for grades, popularity, or attention at home.
Having an older sibling go away to school, move out, or get married. Missing them when they are gone.
Having a sibling who tells lies about you.
Worrying about who your brother/sister chooses for friends and who they go out with (and they think you don't care about them).
Having older siblings blow up at you for "every little thing."
Having younger siblings who want to tag along with you and your friends.
Having to baby-sit for younger siblings.
Being compared with your brothers and sisters; having others expect you to be just like them, good or bad.

Refusing to share.
Sharing the telephone.
Tattling.
Being asked so many questions!
Having an unfair distribution of chores.
Having brothers or sisters who won't listen to you and won't
   be your friend.
Having to set a good example for younger siblings.

Family life today brings challenges. Learning to communicate and get along with parents or brothers and sisters has its times of stress, but also its times of specialness. Even though your family portrait may not tell the behind-the-scenes story at your house, your efforts to improve your family life will pay off.

Express Yourself

What are your family-related stresses? Parents' expectations, their ability to love, divorce, single-parent living, parents dating, lack of trust, bothersome brothers or sisters, other? Identify your stresses and record them here.

Your personal family stresses:

Stress-Relieving Scriptures

Ephesians 6:1–3   Children, obey your parents; this is the right thing to do because God has placed them in authority over you. Honor your father and mother. This is the first of God's Ten Commandments that ends with a promise. And this is the promise: that if you honor your father and mother, yours will be a long life, full of blessing.

Proverbs 1:8, 9   Listen to your father and mother. What you learn from them will stand you in good stead; it will gain you many honors.

Proverbs 13:1 (NAS)   A wise son accepts his father's discipline, but a scoffer does not listen to rebuke.

Psalms 27:10 (NAS)   For my father and my mother have forsaken me, but the Lord will take me up.

John 13:34   And so I am giving a new commandment to you now—love each other just as much as I love you.

7 Friends: Worth the Worry

Debbie told me, "What I enjoy in my friendships is that we are interested in the same things. Take Monica. I always thought I would never be good friends with her. That is, until I found out she loves bargain shopping as much as I do. I know that sounds corny, but we get a rush out of buying thirty-nine-cent nail polish at a K mart blue-light special. We have fun together. Now that I realized we have something in common—dumb as bargain shopping might seem—a whole new friendship has opened up."

Debbie and Monica discovered common ground. From that, their friendship has blossomed. They are more than bargain-hunting partners now, but that is how the relationship started. Whether your similar interest is shopping, academics, roller-skating, building model cars, basketball, fishing, music, or whatever, it's a good way to start and build a new friendship.

Common interests also minimize the stress of trying to find something to do with certain people when you get together. If you don't like similar things, it can put a strain on the time you spend together. Of course, you could challenge yourself and develop a new interest together.

Were there stressful areas of friendship that were reported? Absolutely! That's why friends made the list of top-ten teenage stresses. Let's examine the most frequently reported stresses.

Wanted: Someone Who Needs a Friend as Much as I Do

What does it mean to be a friend? The dictionary definition of the word *friend* reads

> A person attached to another by respect or affection; someone with whom you are not hostile; one who supports or favors someone else.

Someone you respect and who respects you. Someone you are at peace with. Someone who is on your side, stands up for you, believes in you, and prefers you over others. That's a good start in defining a friend.

Friends are also people you can trust. You can share your inner thoughts and feelings with them. You can be honest with them. You are loyal to them. And they are trustworthy, honest, and loyal to you.

Hard to find? Yes. At least that's the way many of the teens I talked to felt.

It's a fact that everyone needs a friend. The stress comes from feeling that you don't have any friends, feeling ignored, feeling unwanted, and feeling that no one cares.

"I get lonely," Kara mumbled with her head down. "I hate admitting that, but I also hate feeling it. Being lonely eats at my insides. I'm afraid to let others get too close. What if they don't like me? Besides, I don't think anyone is interested in being my friend."

Loneliness can result either from not having friends or from having shallow friendships. In his book *Why Am I*

Afraid to Tell You Who I Am? author John Powell addresses Kara's feelings. Someone says to him that he is afraid to tell him who he really is because, "If I tell you who I really am, you may not like me and that is all I have to offer."

This statement is so true. Yet, we can't develop deep friendships if we aren't willing to expose our souls to others. Yes, it's risky and it's stressful, but you may find the risk is better than being friendless or having shallow friendships that consist of nothing more than the normal, "Hi, how are you?" "Oh, I'm fine!" sort of conversations.

Fretting Over Making Friends

Making friends has its stresses, too. Here is what Ryan, Meg, and Teri had to say.

Ryan: "I've always had problems making friends, real friends. Not just having a bunch of guys to hang around with, but one person to open up to. Someone who wouldn't spread around the things we talk about in private."

Meg: "It is hard to make friends when everyone is so preoccupied with being popular and accepted. Why can't we all just be ourselves and quit being fakes? We all have problems, we all have pains. As long as we keep our defenses up, we won't have close friends."

Teri: "I used to think having lots of friends is what was important. I don't think that anymore. It isn't how many friends you have, but how *real* those friendships are. I have one super close friend I can tell everything to. She doesn't laugh at me or put me down. It's so much better to have one friend who listens to you and cares, than fifty so-called friends who couldn't care less what's really going on with you in your life behind the scenes."

Do you ever feel the stress of making friends like these teens do?

Ryan struggles with making what he calls "real

friends." Ryan has discovered that there are various levels of friendship. First there are acquaintances. These are people you say "Hi" to in the hall at school or smile at when you see them in public. Next, there are buddies. These are people you hang around with, maybe just occasionally—a night at the movies, a day surfing or skating—casual interacting. You share your thoughts and ideas with them about nonthreatening topics like school, girls or guys, sports, fashion. Many of these casual friendships can be taken to a deeper level as both people begin to open up.

Then, there are true friends. With these people you are secure enough to talk about your feelings, your dreams, your goals. It is a deeper level of sharing. These are people you probably spend a good amount of time with. They are people you trust.

These are the most fulfilling friendships, the kind of friendship Ryan is looking for. If you have a close friend, great! Treat him or her well. Close friends are rare. If you don't, then go ahead and take the plunge. You may need to be the first one to take your casual friendship to a more personal level.

Meg is feeling frustrated by teens being fake and afraid to be themselves. She realizes that making friends will be hard as long as people keep their defenses up. Meg is very observant. We can't build friendships if we are wearing masks. Everyone hurts and has problems. Acting as if your life is perfect and problem-free is a sure way to keep people at an arm's distance. Sounds like Meg is ready to let down and make a few close friends. How about you?

Teri has made a valuable discovery. The number of friends you have is not as important as the quality of those friendships. Quality counts more than quantity.

A person who is hung up on being popular may not agree that quality counts, but he or she may also feel very alone with no one to talk to. As Teri says, it is better to have one close friend who listens and cares, than fifty so-called friends who are nowhere to be found when you're down.

Being able to make conversation can greatly affect a person's success in making friends. Standing there in dead silence with someone you hardly know is so uncomfortable. So, what do you talk about? Try topics that you have in common like school, parents, where you live, the weather. These are fairly easy topics. Then, ask questions about the person. That shows you are interested in getting to know him. Besides, anyone can talk about himself. In fact, some people are *too* good at it!

Asking other people questions that can't be answered with a quick yes or no is good strategy for getting them to talk longer. Listen to their answers to see if you can pick up on something that could keep the conversation going. Practice with your family members so you will be ready next time you meet someone new. This will help reduce the stress.

Mending the Broken Bond

Fighting, backbiting, jealousy, being two-faced and manipulative—all of these were reported as areas of stress in relation to friends. None of these words is friendly. That is just the point. Things like this are what cause friendships to break up.

Fighting among friends can happen for many reasons. When you are at odds with a friend, life is unpeaceful. Your thoughts are often overtaken by reruns of the last argument you had. It's not good.

Backbiting is a revengeful action people take against someone who has hurt them or threatened them. They speak spitefully against them when they are not there— behind their back.

Jealousy is often the root of these other actions. Jealousy is commonly called the green-eyed monster, and it really *can* become a monster if it is not nipped in the bud. Jealousy ruins friendships and builds walls between people faster than anything.

Two-faced. No, we're not talking about an imaginary freak in a sideshow at the circus! Being two-faced is generally defined as acting friendly to a person's face, then talking against them to others. It's being a fake. It's when someone pretends to like you, then spreads rumors around about what a rotten person you are. Is this a cause for broken friendship? Yes.

Manipulation. When someone bribes you into something or backs you into a corner so you have no choice but to do what they want, you are being manipulated. Or perhaps you have manipulated others. Forcing friends to do what you want won't make for close relationships.

These are not the only things that break friendships. But the important thing here is to realize the amount of stress these actions cause in relationships. It is not fun to go to school dreading the thought of running into someone you have hurt or been hurt by.

You know, the enemy, Satan, wants to keep friendships broken, to keep people apart, to cheat us out of meaningful friendships. Not God, though. He believes in friendship.

Well, what are we to do about broken friendships? Mend them. It won't be easy, but it will be worth it. The key is forgiveness. It takes a special person to be loving enough to forgive. If you think you can't do it, rely on God to help you.

Mending your broken friendships will relieve much of the stress you feel. It allows you to love again, to be filled with joy and to be at peace.

Other Friendly Stresses

You mean there are more? Oh, yes. In fact, there were a lot more stresses reported in the area of friendship. I know you can identify with some of these. Check them out.

Use things, not people. Feeling you are being used by others or willfully using others and feeling guilty about it is stressful. But perhaps the real stress comes from using someone and *not* feeling guilty about it.

Cutting remarks. Teasing put-downs that really do hurt your feelings are a stress that comes from being involved with others. Some kids do their best not to show that they are hurt. But that doesn't alleviate the pain.

Competition. Competing with your friends—whether it's in academics, sports, clothes, or for dates—weakens friendships. Be on the same side!

Being a friend. Some teens really don't know how to be a friend to someone else. Looking out for yourself is so popular in our world. It doesn't teach much about the principles of friendship. Friends don't hurt each other just to get ahead in this world.

Feeling valued. Teens want to be valued by their friends. One girl shared that she thinks it is important to work at making the friendship special. When you treat it special you will value it more. Friends, true friends, make you feel valuable.

Ending friendships. Some teens felt stressed because there were some friendships they wanted to end. They were unsure of how to gracefully end the friendship without deeply hurting the other person. Some friendships end naturally. You may be friends with someone in junior high, but when you move up into high school you go your separate ways and establish new friendships.

Trusting. Teenagers want someone they can trust. It is

usually a prerequisite for a lasting friendship. Sharing your private thoughts with someone who then tells someone else is a major stress. Broken trust hurts. It is not fun to feel betrayed.

Being too busy. Being so busy that you don't have time for your friends can be stressful—especially if the other person does have time. It was also reported that wanting to spend more time with your friends than with your family often caused conflicts.

Friendships can bring stress into our lives because our friends are human. People aren't perfect! Even though we may struggle in our relationships, friends are worth having. God did not intend for us to be islands. We need each other.

Express Yourself

What are your friend-related stresses? Making friends, keeping them, finding common interests, developing meaningful relationships, competing with your friends, others? Identify and record your stresses here.

Your personal friendship stresses:

Stress-Relieving Scriptures

Proverbs 17:17	A true friend is always loyal, and a brother is born to help in time of need.
Proverbs 17:9	Love forgets mistakes; nagging about them parts the best of friends.
1 Corinthians 15:33 (NAS)	Do not be deceived: "Bad company corrupts good morals."
Ephesians 4:32 (NAS)	And be kind to one another, tenderhearted, forgiving each other, just as God in Christ also has forgiven you.
Proverbs 11:13	A gossip goes around spreading rumors, while a trustworthy man tries to quiet them.

8 D-D-D-Dating

Dating and stress go hand in hand. If you have one, you'll have the other.

When asked what stresses her the most about guys, Robin answered, "Guys? Just the way they are stresses me." Well, that about sums it up: the way they are! And what did Glenn have to say about girls? "They're so hard to figure out. Frankly, they are just a pain." Their message

is clear—for girls, guys are hard to understand, and for guys, girls are hard to understand. This keeps dating quite interesting! Girls and guys are very different from each other, as if you hadn't noticed. That's why they are called the opposite sex. It's exactly what they are—*opposite*.

If he's in the mood for roughhousing, she's in the mood for romance. If he's ready for some serious football watching, she'll want to watch her favorite sitcom. She'll want to walk and talk for hours; he'll walk and talk, but only about things like school, sports, his friends. None of that personal stuff—like feelings! She'll want to spend Saturday at the mall shopping and running into all of her friends so they can see her with her guy; he'll want to hang out at the video store sharpening his skills.

Opposite? Very! Yet, God designed us that way. Only opposites are able to complement, balance, and sharpen each other. If guys and girls acted, thought, and felt the same, there would be no complementing, no balancing, no challenge, and no excitement.

And no stress, you say. Well, less stress perhaps. But if your life was completely stress-free you would either be desperately bored or desperately dead! Better check your pulse. If you're alive and normal, your pulse will be beating. If it's beating especially fast, watch out. That special girl or guy who gets your blood pumpin' must be close by!

Scrambling of the Tongue and Brain

"It happens every time she comes over to talk to me," explains Brad. "I can't think of anything smart to say, which doesn't matter anyway because my mouth gets dry and I'm all tongue-tied so that I couldn't get anything intelligent out if I tried."

Poor Brad. We've all been there or will be. Why is it that when the person you have this horrible crush on talks to you, you fall apart? You start losing yourself. First it's your thoughts, then your words, your balance, your composure! You have no problem with the people you don't want to date. But the "other" ones, well—one glance in your direction or a brush of his jacket against yours (or vice versa) and suddenly it's raining from your forehead. Uncontrollable sweat. Go ahead, try to act calm, cool, and collected, if you can.

Remember, not all stress is caused by negative situations. Seeing someone you'd die for, puckering up for your first kiss, or meeting your date's parents can be stressful, but these are usually positive situations. Well, positive as long as you don't really die, you don't miss the lips, and his or her parents don't run you out of the house!

There were many stressful situations reported that relate to dating. Let's look at some of them.

The Big R

Rejection. The word itself makes your heart drop, doesn't it? No one wants to be rejected, yet we all are, at some point. Not everyone you like is going to like you back or ask you out or date you forever! Rejection is one of the pitfalls of dating.

Many of the girls who were surveyed said they weren't stressed by dating because they had never dated. *Wrong!* Not being invited to the prom or some other big event—or even small event—is upsetting to most teenage girls. Let's flip the coin here. Some guys have never asked a girl out. Why? Because they're afraid of getting a no. Rejection. Actually most girls don't give you a flat no. It's usually the baby-sitting excuse they give or the one about already having plans or needing to do their homework. On a Saturday night?

Rejection doesn't have to be devastating. Think about it. Why go out with someone who doesn't want to date you? You are valuable and special. Date someone who appreciates you for who you are!

Most people can handle sitting home on a Friday night, maybe getting together with some friends. But what about the "big nights"? Prom. Homecoming. Winter Formal. New Year's Eve. Valentine's Day.

"I hate missing out. It's not really the dance itself that I miss," says fifteen-year-old Angie, "it's the next day at school. All the girls are in a huddle talking about everything that happened at the dance. They brag about what they wore, who came with who, and all of that. It's exciting. That's what I miss out on."

Steve shared his point of view. "I wish there wasn't so much emphasis on couples at our school. There wasn't anyone I truly wanted to take to the dance, so I get punished by not being able to go at all. That's not fair."

Going alone is not very popular, though it could become popular if more kids would do it. Maybe fewer people would feel rejected on these big nights.

The ultimate rejection, as some teens put it, is breaking up. You've dated for a while, maybe a long while. You've opened up, trusted, really allowed this person to know you. Then, something happens. You drift apart. Maybe he wants to get too sexual. Maybe she wants to get too serious. Whatever the cause, the breakup occurs. Rejection. Stress. Pain.

There are many reasons breaking up is so stressful. Yes, you feel rejected. You feel embarrassed. You wonder what people will say, if anyone will ever ask you out again, if you and your "ex" will ever be friends again.

Stress from breaking up can be so upsetting that sometimes people change schools, drop out, run away, get very sick, or even think about ending their lives. Let me tell you this, as one who has already been through all the dating devastations—there *is* life after a major breakup! Though you can't concentrate on anything else and your heart feels like it's ripping out, the pain, the stress, the worries do go away.

Whenever you feel rejected, it's a good time to put your prayer power into effect. Tell the Lord how you feel. Allow Him to heal your hurts.

Psalm 34:18 tells us the Lord is near to the brokenhearted. He is there to comfort you, console you, ease your mind, and calm your stress. Jesus knows what rejection feels like. To Him, the ultimate rejection led to His death. Yet, He endured it because He loved. And one person He loves is you. Reach out to Him when you hurt. His Band-Aids are the best!

The Big V

Virginity. Of course, I'm talking about keeping it, not losing it! I'm sorry this is such an issue for teens, especially Christian teens who desire to be obedient to the Lord. Sex is a sacred, loving interaction that was designed by a loving God to be experienced within the security of a marriage. Sex has been so abused by the world.

Pam shared, "Guys can't understand that I really just want to be friends and not feel like I have to have sex to keep them happy. Guys should be happy they are dating someone who doesn't sleep around."

Dan is concerned. "'I am a seventeen-year-old virgin and I want to marry a virgin. I suppose there are some girls out there right now who are still virgins, too. But what about when I'm twenty-five and start seriously wanting a wife. Will there be any virgins left?"

"Everybody's doing it. That's what I always hear," said Sherry. "But it's not true. I'm not doing it, so everybody is not doing it. I know that some of my friends are having sex and it upsets me. If their boyfriends had any respect for them and the girls had any respect for themselves, they wouldn't do it. They are just being used and will end up hurt." Sherry continues, "That's when they come to me, to comfort them and tell them everything will be okay. But I'm not doing that anymore. They are being stupid by having sex. It's never going to be okay as long as they keep making bad choices. I refuse to keep patching them together when they keep ripping themselves apart."

Three legitimate stresses. Pam feels the pressure of a boyfriend who wants her to compromise herself and give in to his requests for sex. Dan is concerned that there won't be any virgins left when he wants to get married. Sherry feels angry that people try to make her believe that everyone is sexually active. She is angry at her friends for not respecting themselves enough to say no to sex before marriage. After all, she is tired of being the one they run to for assurance that everything's okay.

Society tells us that sex before marriage is okay, it's natural, no big deal. Premarital sex is treated too casually. The Bible tells us something else. It doesn't just suggest you refrain from premarital sex—it requires it. God's instruction is there for your protection. To protect you from what?—from emotional pain, from contracting one or several of the twenty-some sexually transmitted diseases like gonorrhea, herpes, chlamydia, or—the big one—AIDS! Abstaining will also protect you from an unplanned pregnancy, from inflicting a blow to your self-image, and will protect your relationship with Him. Premarital sex is a sin. It is something to confess and repent of.

Yes, there is stress in saying no to sexual involvement. It may mean losing a boyfriend, not having many dates, or being teased for being a prude. But that kind of stress is mild compared to the fear of pregnancy or contracting an incurable disease or the awful feeling of running into someone you used to sleep with. Many Christians suffer from the self-disgust they experience when they have compromised this area of their lives. The Lord can help. This is stress that can be avoided.

The Big M

Marriage. Believe it or not, there is a sane purpose for dating. It is to discover the type of personality, the qualities, the characteristics, and the values of the person you want to someday spend the rest of your life with. Dating assists you in pinpointing your wants and needs in a life partner. Not that you'll be able to fill every requirement on your list, but it gives you direction.

One of the stresses reported was the stress of searching for the right person. It takes prayer, patience, and persistence. You may have to endure many dates and kiss a toad or two, but don't give up or sell yourself short!

When you are patient and wait for the right spouse, your fear of another major stress—divorce—will not be as great. First of all, find someone who is a Christian and believes as you do that divorce is not an option. Then don't let it be part of your vocabulary. Every marriage goes through rough, rocky times and getting out of the relationship seems to be the easiest option. But if you are committed, you can work things out. There is not a problem too big for God. Don't get me wrong, there are legitimate grounds for divorce, but if you go into your marriage wondering if you'll get a divorce, you probably won't try as hard to make it last. Trust the Lord.

More Dastardly Dating Stresses

We briefly discussed a few of the many stresses of dating. Here are a few more that can't go unmentioned.

Wrong person. Being asked out by the best friend of the guy or girl that you really want to go out with—now that can bring stress. What about when the person you are hoping to date starts going out with your best friend? Sticky!

Prejudging. If the person you are dating is not considered "cool," others may prejudge him or her. How unfair. Don't be influenced by others. It will be their loss when they realize that you have discovered a diamond in the rough.

Possessiveness. Dating a person who wants to be with you all of the time is rough. Help! You may not be able to breathe! Usually the possessive person is also jealous.

Respect. Several girls reported that they wanted to be treated like a lady instead of one of the guys.

Betrayal. It hurts to find out your boyfriend or girlfriend really likes someone else or has dated someone else behind your back.

The real you. Do you wonder if you will ever meet

someone who likes you just because you are you? No masks, no games. Some teens lose self-esteem because the person they like doesn't like them back. It is wasted effort trying to *make* someone like you.

Christian inside and out. Trying to find people to go out with who act like Christians even on a date can be a challenge!

Pressure to compromise. Pressure to do things that are not right or even illegal just because the group you are with is doing them is stressful. A date, a boyfriend, or a girlfriend is not worth ending up in jail for.

Parents. It can be upsetting when parents don't want you to date until you are a certain age, like sixteen or so. This is where group dates come in handy. They also take a lot of pressure off being alone with one person. Parents are also good at setting curfews. Curfews can be a curse if yours is two hours earlier than everyone else's. But parents need to be given more credit. Following their rules has kept many kids from dangerous situations.

I think I'm in love. When you are head over heels for someone, it's hard to know if you are really in love or just infatuated. New love is always exciting. Sometimes teens get carried away thinking they have found their one true love. Yet, teen romances almost never become permanent. It's too hard to know what you want in a mate when you are still deciding what you want in yourself.

A different stress that was reported in this area is the frustration teens feel when their parents don't take them seriously about their feelings toward their boyfriend or girlfriend. It was also reported that teens feel like they don't know how to define love. Some kids thought it was a feeling; some said love is a commitment. Both are right. Love is a combination of the two, with a little extra weight on the commitment side. Goosebumpy feelings of love are not always present in any relationship. Check out 1 Corinthians 13:4–7 for the real definition of love.

Stamp of approval. Some parents want to get to know the person their teen dates. They may require that he or she pass their approval test. This can be a frustration, but important to your parents.

Dating adds good and bad stress to your teenage life. The fun and the heartbreak can take their toll. But as you date you'll begin to see what qualities are important to you in a life partner. That makes the stress a little more bearable.

Express Yourself

What are your dating-related stresses? Being shy and tongue-tied around the opposite sex, rejection, keeping your virginity, wondering about marriage, having dates, going to the prom, being betrayed, falling in love? Identify and record your stresses here.

Your personal dating stresses:

Stress-Relieving Scriptures

2 Timothy 2:22 (NAS)	Now flee from youthful lusts, and pursue righteousness, faith, love and peace, with those who call on the Lord from a pure heart.
Hebrews 12:16	Watch out that no one becomes involved in sexual sin or becomes careless about God. . . .
1 Thessalonians 4:3, 4	For God wants you to be holy and pure, and to keep clear of all sexual sin so that each of you will marry in holiness and honor.
Genesis 2:18	And the Lord God said, "It isn't good for man to be alone; I will make a companion for him, a helper suited to his needs."
1 Corinthians 13:4–7	Love is very patient and kind, never jealous or envious, never boastful or proud, never haughty or selfish or rude. Love does not demand its own way. It is not irritable or touchy. It does not hold grudges and will hardly even notice when others do it wrong. It is never glad about injustice, but rejoices whenever truth wins out. If you love someone you will be loyal to him no matter what the cost. You will always believe in him, always expect the best of him, and always stand your ground in defending him.

9 The Popularity Puzzle

Is popularity a major cause of stress for today's teens? You be the judge.

"Just hearing the word stresses me," reports high school student Katie. "When I think of all the phoniness that goes along with popularity I want to be sick."

John shares, "I know I'm not popular. I'm sort of in the middle group. I'm okay. But I don't like that feeling very much. At least I know that to God I'm more than average. Our society sets up unfair measuring sticks."

Gwynn told me, "After watching the problems of most of the popular kids at my school, I don't want to be popular. I'm not popular by choice. I really don't want the pressures that go along with being in the 'in' group."

Beth was very sure about how she felt. "I have a few close friends, not a lot, but at least I know they really are my friends. Sure, I've always wanted to be popular, but I'll settle for knowing I'm popular just with my friends."

"The thing that stresses me the most about the whole issue of popularity," said Bill, "is that I've always wanted to fit in and feel like I belong, so I had to find the right group to do that with. I'm not that popular in the whole school, but in my own group I am. That way, I feel respected by the other kids."

Popularity and what's involved with it definitely rate on the anxiety list. I still haven't forgotten my own stress over popularity while I was in high school. I remember walking past the lounge area of our high school known as "the commons." It's that certain place that every school has where the "in" kids congregate in the morning before school starts. Stand and observe for only a moment and you'll know the whole story. Who is popular, who is not. Who is trying to be popular, but not having much luck. Who doesn't care if they are popular. Interesting.

Notice I said I remember *walking past* the commons? Only once during my high school years did I feel "allowed" to sit or hang around that area. It was my junior year. I happened to be dating a good-looking guy from a school across town. The popular girls from my school knew he was popular at his school, so suddenly I was included and invited into the "in" group. It was great for a while. People who had never talked to me before were friendly. Of course there was next to nothing to say since I was not the same type of person they were. But I got invited to parties that only the most popular teens got to go to.

My sudden popularity came to a screeching halt one day when the guy I was dating decided he wanted to "date around." And who did he want to date? One of the other girls in the "in" group at my school.

Those friendly smiles of my new group of "friends" stopped smiling. In fact, most of these girls wouldn't even look at me when we passed in the halls between classes. And stand in the commons before school? Not anymore. I don't know if guys act this way, but girls can sure be hateful toward each other.

That whole experience left me feeling rejected and angry. But through it all I learned some important truths, some of the very things that were reported on the questionnaires. I used to think I was missing out on something really great. I wasn't; the parties were no big deal. I also learned the value of real friendship.

The only other time those popular girls paid attention to me was in my senior year. I had gotten very involved with modeling and was on the fashion board of a large department store (sort of a big deal where we lived) as the representative from our high school. Then, I was selected as Madison's Junior Miss (Madison is in Wisconsin). Those girls decided these were reasons enough for putting their seal of approval on me once again.

This time when they invited me to their gatherings, I graciously declined. When they tried to butter me up and act like we were long-lost buddies, I was courteous, but didn't participate. I knew I didn't need their acceptance anymore.

We all want to know that we are okay. We can easily get stressed over thinking we're not good enough or that no one likes us. Katie, John, Gwynn, Beth, and Bill all expressed different stresses they felt because of popularity. They are all causes worth looking at.

Being Yourself

Katie is really put off by the phony way some people act when they are, or think they are, popular. They want everyone to like them so they try to be what everyone else wants them to be. They may know nothing about you but act like you've been pals forever. These kinds of people may never learn how to just be themselves or how to like themselves.

Katie felt it was better to be real and to be honest with others than to be a fake.

I have a friend who recently graduated from high school. She was quite popular—not because she was a cheerleader, a class officer, incredibly attractive, or best dressed. My friend Kelly was popular because she was confident in just being herself around campus.

Kelly was from a well-off family, but wouldn't show it with her clothes. She wore sweatsuits most of the time and was notorious for showing up at places in her slippers. Kelly didn't wear makeup and wore her hair plain. She was good at encouraging people and caring about how they were doing. This quality of Kelly's was especially evident with her swim team. You could count on Kelly to be out there congratulating each girl on her team who just finished a race . . . whether she won or lost!

Kelly was always smiling. Not because she was trying to impress anyone, but because she was happy. No, her life wasn't perfect or easy, but she had learned to take life as it comes and look for the good in all situations. She also loved the Lord and allowed His love to shine through her to the other kids at school. She didn't associate just with certain students. She talked to everyone.

Kelly was popular. Popular for the right reasons. She was confident to be herself and to let others see her for what she was. If someone didn't like her, it was okay.

During her senior year, Kelly was nominated for the Homecoming Court. It was an honor for her, but mostly she thought it was funny. And when she was actually crowned Homecoming Queen? She couldn't help but smile and laugh.

Kelly was popular because she was herself. Her acceptance of herself wasn't based on whether or not the teenagers at school liked her. It was based on the love and acceptance she felt from herself, her Lord, and her family.

You, too, can let the Lord's love and acceptance be your basis for learning to be yourself. You don't have to live your life behind a mask or try to maintain an image. Just be yourself.

Popular With God

John sensed that on a popularity scale from 1–10, he was about a 5 or 6. He described himself as an average guy who wasn't particularly well-known. I agree with his statement about our society setting up unfair measuring sticks. A person isn't more valuable just because he or she is popular. What about the teenager who goes to the children's ward of the hospital to visit sick children every other afternoon? That isn't being popular on campus, but he is sure important to those kids. He is valued by them. The other people at school may not know what you do in your private world. So they are poor judges of your personal value.

John also felt stressed over being considered average—sort of fitting into the middle group, as he described it. Labels are unfair. The way others classify a person may be completely wrong. Sometimes it's a struggle to convince them otherwise. John had a good attitude, though. "At least I know that to God, I'm more than average." And he is right.

Popular Problems

Gwynn had watched the kids at her school. It seemed that the popular ones were always having extra problems—whether it was dating traumas or getting in trouble at a party. She didn't want those troubles. Nor did she want to get petty about what she wore to school every day. She didn't like feeling that she needed to compete with the others. There were other things to put her attention on besides herself. Gwynn didn't want the stress and pressure that goes along with popularity.

Peer pressure tries to force teens to do things they may not want to do. Sometimes it's a perceived pressure; other times it's someone actually handing you a wine cooler and telling you that you're a baby if you don't drink it. Maybe it's someone threatening to beat you up if you don't give him the test answers or promise to pass him the football in Friday night's big game.

We think of peer pressure as negative. Traditionally, it has been. But today, kids are pushing positive peer pressure. They are turning the tables and making it the cool thing *not* to take drugs or drink or engage in premarital sex or steal or whatever. Maybe you could get a group together at your school and start some positive peer pressure. It sure helps relieve some of the stress!

Just a Few Close Friends

Beth was very up-front about her thoughts. She had wanted to be popular. When it comes to popularity, Beth realized that it was quality not quantity that counted. She had learned the value of having a few close friends who cared, instead of many acquaintances.

Beth's life was more stressful when she wanted to be popular with everyone than it is now that she has one or two close friends who are always on her side.

Needing to Belong

One area of stress tied in with popularity is the need to belong. We all need to feel connected with something. This is what Bill had experienced. He wanted to fit in and feel like part of the group.

Bill was very talented in drama. He enrolled in all the acting, stage production, and theater classes at school. His talent developed quickly. He won the leads in most of the plays and performed well. He especially enjoyed the other students in drama. He felt he fit in with them. Because he was good at what he did, he felt respected by the other students on campus, even though they weren't really his friends. Guess you could say he was popular among his own group.

As you develop your personality, talents, interests, goals, and beliefs, you'll begin to see where your niche in life is. If you're at a stage in life where you don't feel like you belong to anyone or anything, let me assure you of this: If you have invited Jesus Christ to come into your life to be your Lord and Savior, then you belong to Him. You are part of the family of God—the biggest family there is! God has placed gifts and talents in each of us and, in time, you will see exactly what yours are! Then you can develop them and use them for Him.

Additional "Popular" Stresses

Cliques. Many teens said that cliques stressed them. These small exclusive groups have a way of making you feel either left out or included. Cliques are hard to break. Teens get stuck with their little group of friends and sometimes aren't open to including others. This is especially hard on new or shy students. Some students disliked cliques because of their fear of being left out. It's not fun to eat lunch alone. Some teens want to be in cliques to feel included.

Popularity musts! Several kids shared that they felt they *must* date a popular guy or girl, they *must* be popular to be respected and recognized, and they *must* be in sports, dress the best, and live up to a certain image. Go ahead, be a *must buster!*

Popularity-possessed. Several teens thought that being popular was so important that they actually spent time thinking of ways to become more popular and planning out strategies to ensure the success of their popularity campaign. Sounds stressful.

Misunderstood. Teens who are shy are often misinterpreted as being in a bad mood or as being stuck-up. This certainly limits their popularity potential.

Stuck in the stereotype. Teens who are naturally well-liked, like Kelly, find themselves in the popular crowd. Some of these popular people felt that their peers don't give them a chance to be their friends because of the stereotype of most popular teens. These peers think the

popular person is just trying to win himself one more
vote.

Being popular and well liked are the desires of most
teens, but if it becomes your aim, watch out! One step
better than popularity is being yourself and being popular with God. He is on your cheering team. In His eyes,
you *are* number one.

Express Yourself

What are your popularity-related stresses? Wanting to
be popular, phoniness, being yourself, being popular
with God, peer pressure, needing to belong, others?
Identify and record your stresses here.

Your personal popularity stresses:

Stress-Relieving Scriptures

Proverbs 18:24   There are "friends" who pretend to be friends, but there is a friend who sticks closer than a brother.

Luke 6:31   Treat others as you want them to treat you.

Romans 12:16   Work happily together. Don't try to act big. Don't try to get into the good graces of important people, but enjoy the company of ordinary folks. And don't think you know it all!

Philippians 2:3, 4 Don't be selfish; don't live to make a good impression on others. Be humble, thinking of others as better than yourself. Don't just think about your own affairs, but be interested in others, too, and in what they are doing.

10 Self-Image

Your self-image is based on the way you see yourself and the way you feel about yourself. Self-image is the foundation you build yourself upon. It may fluctuate a bit depending on whether you have a good day or a bad day.

A healthy self-image is very valuable. It can affect your life goals, your dating relationships, even your marriage choice. With a good self-image you can get further in life and feel good about who you have become. With a bad self-image you may not get where you want to go. Life can become a dreaded chore if you don't like yourself.

The great thing is that self-image can be changed! You can develop a good self-image and a healthy love and appreciation for yourself.

Having a poor self-image causes stress—stress over not liking yourself, thinking others don't like you, feeling you don't measure up. A good majority of teens have a self-image problem. Here are a few of the main areas of self-image that stress teenagers.

Appearance

Robbie was tall and rather thin for his age. He could see over the heads of nearly every other kid at his new high school.

"How's the weather up there?" and "Hey, stringbean, are you related to the Jolly Green Giant?" were familiar questions to him. He knew people were teasing, but he didn't appreciate their cheap jabs.

Even on the basketball court—where it's normal to find tall, thin guys—Robbie got teased. Still in a growing stage of life, his coordination hadn't quite caught up with his latest spurt of growth. Once he tripped and fell over his own feet and his glasses flew across the court. The cheerleaders giggled, but not him. He couldn't stand them. They flocked after the guys with bulging, fine-tuned muscles and suntans. Compared to the other jocks, Robbie felt inferior, and it was wearing on his self-image.

Physical appearance is one of the leading causes of stress related to self-image. If you stop to think about it, it's no wonder why!

Our society blasts us with its idea of the perfect man and the perfect woman. For guys, it's arm and chest muscles, a tight derriere, tousled hair, and squared jawbone. It's an Arnold Schwarzenegger body and a Tom Cruise face.

Girls, you certainly don't have it any easier. Clear flawless skin, thin, fat-free body with a hint of muscle tone, straight white teeth, cute little nose—a total cover girl. For you, it's a Jane Fonda body and a Christie Brinkley face.

Okay. Sure. No problem. WRONG!

Our society values such phony qualities and characteristics. How can it be more important to have blond hair and blue eyes than to have a caring heart and a loving, helpful attitude? It's twisted. Our society's standards are impossible to meet. No wonder Robbie and many others get stressed over their appearance. Comparing your looks to others will only increase your anxiety.

Leanne had a habit of comparing. One day it would be her nails (too short), then her eyes (too squinty), then her lips (too full), her legs (too thick), her clothes (not new), and on and on. Leanne didn't stand a chance with herself! Comparing yourself with others, especially if you think everyone else is better than you are, can leave you down in the dumps.

Life is happier when you learn to love yourself just as you are. Change things that can be changed like weight, hairstyle, or teeth, but accept the others. You will be less stressed and your self-image will improve.

For further insight on self-image in relation to appearance, I refer the girls to my book *Beautifully Created*.

Confidence

Several teens reported that what stressed them was their lack of confidence.

Confidence means having faith or belief. To have confidence in yourself means to believe in yourself, have faith in you! Build your confidence by attempting new things, trying a little harder, and relying on the Lord to help you.

Your confidence doesn't have to be just in yourself. It can be in the Lord too! Proverbs 3:26 (NAS) says that "the Lord will be your confidence. . . ." Put your trust in Jesus and ask Him to give you confidence.

Sally told me she lacked confidence in herself and that her life wouldn't amount to anything. As Christians we have an additional confidence. In Philippians 1:6 Paul says he is confident that God had begun a good work in the believers and that He would continue to perfect what He started until the time we die or Jesus comes to earth to get us. That's forever! We can be confident that Jesus is working in us and through us to accomplish what He wants us to do and be!

Perfectionism

One way to guarantee stress in your life is to expect yourself to be perfect! If you expect perfection (which you'll never achieve), you will set yourself up for failure. What will happen to your self-image? It will get rained on!

No one is perfect. I don't care how together somebody appears to be, there's bound to be a loose end somewhere. Maybe they've just gotten good at hiding those frayed ends!

Cathy thought she needed to be perfect. She set high standards for herself and compared herself with girls whom she considered to be striving toward perfection. But the same thing always happened, she kept falling short. Her stress was showing up in her cranky attitude toward everyone and her inability to sleep at night.

A friend of Cathy's mom, Lois, noticed the changes in Cathy. She was able to help Cathy pinpoint the cause of her stress: perfectionism.

Lois helped Cathy see that she had both strengths and weaknesses. That's normal; no one is good at everything. Life became less of a struggle to Cathy when she started accepting her strengths and weaknesses. She realized that a balanced, well-rounded Cathy was happier than a stressed Cathy striving to be something she couldn't.

More Self-Image Stresses

Embarrassing moments. Do embarrassing moments make you want to crawl into a hole? Most kids said school was the prime place for embarrassing mishaps. Dropping your books all over, having a chair pulled out from under you, being called to the principal's office, having your mom drop your sack lunch off in the attendance

office, or how about when you ask someone out and she
or he says no, and you later run into that person on a date
with someone else. How about getting fired from a job or
getting pulled over by a police officer. Stressful! Embarrassing moments go hand in hand with sweat! They are
no good at boosting your self-confidence.

Living through puberty. Oh, yeah—*puberty*. A time
when those hidden hormones start kicking in. A time
when self-consciousness runs rampant. A time when
you question the wisdom of God's design. Fretting over
your body development, your voice change, your height,
your menstrual cycle, your facial hair won't make the
transition any smoother. Be assured you are not in the
puberty pond alone—every other kid at school is stressed
out about this, too!

Bursting with brains. Brains are one of the three *B*'s that
our society inflates—beauty, brains, bucks. Many teens
felt uptight over their level of intelligence. "I wish I was
smarter!" was a frequent desire.

Compromising standards. Doing things that are not in
line with your beliefs causes a great deal of stress. Especially when you feel as if you have disappointed yourself,
your parents, your friends, or God. Keeping your con-
science clear is an effective stress reducer!

Feeling valued. When you feel valued by those who are
important to you, life is smoother. If you don't feel valued by others, know that God values you greatly. He
matters most!

When your self-image is based on God's love for you
and His opinion of you, it will be healthy and balanced.
God has designed you in a special way and has a plan for
your life. Learning to love yourself will help those self-
image stresses fade away.

Express Yourself

What are your stresses relating to your self-image?
Disliking your appearance, lacking confidence, self-

doubt, expecting yourself to be perfect, others? Identify and record your stresses here.

Your personal self-image stresses:

Stress-Relieving Scriptures

1 Samuel 16:7 (NAS)	. . . For God sees not as man sees, for man looks at the outward appearance, but the Lord looks at the heart.
Psalm 71:5 (NAS)	For Thou art my hope; O Lord God, Thou art my confidence from my youth.
Psalm 139:13, 14	You made all the delicate, inner parts of my body, and knit them together in my mother's womb. Thank you for making me so wonderfully complex! It is amazing to think about. Your workmanship is marvelous—and how well I know it.
2 Corinthians 3:4, 5 (NAS)	And such confidence we have through Christ toward God. Not that we are adequate in ourselves to consider anything as coming from ourselves, but our adequacy is from God.
2 Corinthians 2:14 (NAS)	But thanks be to God, who always leads us in His triumph in Christ, and manifests through us the sweet aroma of the knowledge of Him in every place.

11 Money Matters

Money. Why is it so unfair? Why is it so necessary? Why does it have so much power? Money causes more problems than you'd think possible for a thin piece of dark green paper. Problems, not just for adults, but for teens as well.

Teens wonder, who gave money the right to say who is rich or who is poor? who will have Guess jeans, who will have Lee? who will drive a brand-new car or who will drive a used clunker? who will be considered upper class and who will be considered lower?

The causes of stress in relation to money varied in reports from teens, but all are legitimate. Want to know the biggest cause of money stress for teens?

Not Having Any!

There it is in their own words! *Not having any!* And their reasons for not having any?

"I don't have a job so I haven't earned any."

"I seem to spend every penny I get and always end up broke."

"Don't ask me how, but I lose it."

"My parents stopped giving me an allowance when I became old enough to work, but I don't like to work."

Whatever the reason the result was the same—empty pockets! Exactly what do teenagers need money for? You probably don't have to think too long to come up with an answer to that question. How about clothes, shoes, movies, romance novels, magazines, dates, gas, snacks, haircuts, basketball shoes, uniforms, or car and insurance payments?

College money is always a biggie. Some kids start trying to save money while in high school. Others panic and fill out every financial aid form available, praying that they will get funded. Most do both!

We live in a privileged society where almost anyone can earn money. So, if your piggy bank is empty, work is always an option.

Working Teens

Easier said than done! One of the stresses of working is finding the time. Many kids are involved with school, sports, clubs, or community activities. Taking on a job means a busier schedule or eliminating an activity.

Another stress is actually getting a job. Fifteen-year-old Jane said, "I get so nervous when I apply for a job, I feel like I say the wrong things." Job interviews are sure to get those palms sweating and stomachs churning! Presenting yourself well, speaking clearly, and on-the-spot thinking can be a challenge.

"My money-related stress is budgeting," Todd reported. This is a major concern for many. Earning, saving, and spending your money wisely takes self-control. It means saying no to some of the fun little trinkets and saving for more sensible purchases.

"I'm not qualified to do much right now. So I deliver papers. I'm glad I won't do this forever, but for now it's working out very well," says paperboy Don. It's true. When you are young, you haven't developed many marketable skills. Be patient, you're sure to develop a few in the future. Or be creative, start your own lawn care, baby-sitting, housecleaning, or grocery delivery service!

Bitten by Jealousy

"I have an inner conflict. I don't want to be jealous, but I see other people who have lots of money and are totally careless with it. I just wish it were me," remarked Joshua.

Anna adds, "Yeah. When I get jealous of someone, I get angry. Why should they have what I can't? I get so mad, I refuse to be their friend."

Jealousy never breeds goodness. In Joshua's case, he got stressed because of his inner argument. He felt jealous, but he knew he should feel happy and grateful for what he did have. Good point! In the Bible, the apostle Paul tells us he learned to be content in all his situations—including whether or not he had any finances.

Anna's jealousy is causing her extra pressure when she gets angry with others and decides not to be their friend. Anger takes more energy out of a person that any other emotion.

More Money Causes of Stress

Almost every teen responded on the questionnaire to the money and work questions. Here are a few more causes of their stress on this highly tense topic.

Money from Mom and Dad. Some teens assume their parents will give them money. Some parents do, but not all of them.

Empty-wallet syndrome. All of your friends are planning to meet at the theater tonight. You say you can't come along. They all ask you why. Quick, you need an excuse! Ever been in this situation? Most kids don't want to say they don't have the money, but usually, your friends will understand.

Keeping a job. Now that you've gotten the job, keeping it is the key. Some teens felt their jobs were boring. Some worked at the same place as their friends. Well, if your boredom has you sloughing off, or your social life has affected your work performance, you could find yourself back in the unemployed status once again.

Working attitude. Continually being kind and courteous to the customers is challenging. Having to be Pleasant Polly or Courteous Curt gets old, especially if you are not in the best of moods. This can be a good time to practice being loving.

Baby-sitting. If you don't have the time to hold a job after school or on weekends, you may find your main source of income is baby-sitting. Baby-sitting can be a stress when you also have younger brothers and sisters at home.

Pleasing the boss. This is a tough one. If you have a tough boss, just thinking about work can make you hyper.

Restlessness. One student reported that he couldn't stand being at one job too long. He lost interest rapidly. He has switched jobs so many times, it was making it hard for him to get hired. His past record looked suspicious.

Perspective on money. Yes, keeping money in perspective can be a challenge. Some people are driven by their desire to make lots of money. One teen shared that he loves money but doesn't want money to own him.

Money is meant to be used to supply our needs and we can trust God to provide money through His means for us. Money itself is not evil, but if a person loves money, it causes evil in his heart. Trust God to supply your needs.

Express Yourself

What are your money-related stresses? Not enough money, getting and keeping a job, adjusting your stan-

dards to your income, being jealous of others' posses-
sions, learning to spend wisely, others? Identify and
record your stresses here.

Your personal money stresses:

Stress-Relieving Scriptures

Proverbs 23:4 (NAS)	Do not weary yourself to gain wealth, Cease from your consideration of it.
1 Timothy 6:10	For the love of money is the first step toward all kinds of sin. Some people have even turned away from God because of their love for it, and as a result have pierced themselves with many sorrows.
Psalm 37:16	It is better to have little and be godly than to own an evil man's wealth.
Proverbs 10:22	The Lord's blessing is our greatest wealth. All our work adds nothing to it!
Matthew 6:24	You cannot serve two masters: God and money. For you will hate one and love the other or else the other way around.

12 Fears About the Future

What will life be like in 2010? How will the headlines read?

"NUCLEAR WAR AROUND THE CORNER"
"PRESIDENT DIES OF AIDS"
"MARRIAGE NO LONGER LEGAL"
"COCAINE: NOW AT YOUR LOCAL DRUGSTORE"

Thoughts of the future can be frightening. Our ability to foresee our future or the world's future is limited. People through the years have always been a bit edgy about the unknown. Only God knows what lies ahead for us—as a nation, as a church, as a family, and as individuals. But take heart. The promise in Jeremiah 29:11 offers you new courage and confidence about your future.

> For I know the plans I have for you, says the Lord. They are plans for good and not for evil, to give you a future and a hope.

What a relief. When the questions concerning your future seem to overwhelm you, God has a plan. In the Scripture that we just read, God promises us a future and a hope. Hope is a necessary ingredient when it comes to determining what's ahead for you. If you don't have hope, chances are you will end up spinning your wheels, running in circles, quitting too soon, and going nowhere. When people feel hopeless, their hearts are heavy. They feel useless and find no purpose in life. Jesus says, "Wake up, in Me there is hope and a future for you."

Too many teens today are walking around with no hope. Hope is so vital. It starts in your heart like a tiny seed that is planted deep in the soil. When it begins to sprout, your faith increases; your confidence rises. You start having a vision for yourself. Proverbs 29:18 warns us that without a vision, a dream, a goal, we will perish. Without a vision, people wither up and die on the inside.

As your vision takes form you acquire a sense of direction; your efforts won't be aimless. You know where you're going. Jesus can give you hope and direction, thus relieving your fears of the future.

Which Way Do I Go?

Remember the Scarecrow in *The Wizard of Oz?* When Dorothy first meets him, he seems rather confused. When she asks him which way to the Land of Oz, where the great Wizard lives, he points in two directions. Then when she asks him again, he points in two different directions.

Do you ever feel like the Scarecrow? Many teens reported that they do. Deciding which path to take in your life is a major decision. Today's world offers so many opportunities and choices. Picking a path can be very complicated.

"I've done okay in school," explains Paul, "but I haven't decided whether I should go to college or get a job for a while. Getting a job would give me some time to think about what sort of college degree I want. I really get bugged over these decisions."

Paul represents the most common concern reported on the questionnaires. Many teens felt similar stresses over college, a career, or a job in the future.

"It's tough getting into a good college. I don't know if I can cut it or if I will have the money for college when the time comes."

"Imagining more school blows my mind. I think I need a vacation."

"Teaching sounds good to me, but there's not much money in it."

"I play the violin pretty well. Maybe I'll join an orchestra and become a professional."

"I'm going for the bucks. I want to retire at age thirty."

"Me? I'm going to skip college and marry a rich movie star so I won't have to worry about anything."

A plumber? A businessman? A fashion buyer? A four-year college? A trade school? Graduate school? A career? A job? Making a living? Tough decisions. With a lot of persistence, a lot of prayer, and taking one step at a time, the puzzle will begin to unravel.

Till Death Do You Part: The Fear of Marriage

Forever is a long time. Many teens wonder if they have what it takes to commit themselves to another person that long. With the divorce rate being what it is, marriage has become a future stress. Some teens have seen the beautiful side of marriage, but many have seen their own parents fail at marriage. They have seen hurt, pain, tears, and betrayal.

Divorce was not the only fear reported when the topic of marriage was brought up. Many teens were stressed over the idea of finding the "right" person to marry. Is

Mr. or Miss Wonderful really out there? How will they know when they have found him or her?

All stress in marriage is not bad stress. For instance, the wedding itself is a time when tension runs high, nerves are on edge. The bride wants everything to be perfect, the groom wants to be on time, the mother wants the reception to roll smoothly, the father hopes he can pay for everything. Then, as life progresses, so do the exciting, but stressful events. Like buying your first house or first car. There are loans, payments, and interest rates to take into consideration. And what about a family? Oh, yes. Adding a few babies to the nest. Delivery, hospital bills, clothes, schooling. These are all potentially happy and exciting times, with their own kind of stress.

Will I Be Famous or Floppish?

Once you're out of college and in the work world, the pressure to succeed stares you in the face. At least you may feel that it does. Friends are watching. Employers are watching. Parents are watching. The thought of failing terrifies many teens as they look to their future. Yet, whether you are a success or not depends on how you define the word *success*.

Patti told me, "I think I will feel successful if I am happy. It doesn't matter to me what I am doing or how much money I am making, but if I am smiling, I'm a success."

Jason felt this way: "My dad owns his own company. He is a very successful businessman and quite respected in our city. Following in his footsteps, I feel I had better make something of myself or it will make my dad look like he didn't raise me very well. I do want to make him proud of me."

Mike's viewpoint was that "Success is when all the bills are paid, you have a little extra money for the movies, but most important, you have success when your life is straight with God. If I screw up my life in every other area, it won't matter. My relationship to God is what matters most."

Patti, Jason, and Mike have different ways to measure their future success. The amount of stress they each experience will depend on whether or not they live up to their own standards.

The world's view of success is to be in control, wealthy, educated, good-looking, and putting yourself first. God's view is different. He doesn't pressure us to be millionaires or professors. He challenges us to follow Him. Following Him, we will find success.

Joshua 1:8 (NAS) describes God's formula for success. You may find it helpful.

> This book of the law shall not depart from your mouth, but you shall meditate on it day and night, so that you may be careful to do according to all that is written in it; for then you will make your way prosperous, and then you will have success.

The interesting fact about this verse is that when we obey the Lord and live at peace with Him, He not only makes us prosperous by supplying all our needs, but He also gives us hearts of love and joy. Our success can spread to every area of our life when we let the Lord in and follow His Word!

The Final Curtain

"Hopefully, dying won't happen for a long time," said Joe, "but still, I think about it. I mean, I'm only seventeen, but the thought of dying upsets me. I hope I will live my life 100 percent before that last day comes."

Death. Not a pleasant thought to most teens. Yet, it is

a very real part of life. Many kids have seen their great grandparents or grandparents pass away. Some have endured the pain of losing a parent or a close friend. Death is a reality—and a stressful one.

"I hate pain. I don't want to sound wimpy, but when I die I hope it will be quick and painless," shared Rich.

The fear of pain and the way they may die were some of the most stressful aspects of death that were shared by teens. But these concerns are not limited to teens. Adults have similar fears and worries.

The other fear about death that was most commonly reported was the finality of the question: Is there a heaven and hell? Where will I go?

Even though the majority of the teens questioned were Christians, some still felt unsure about the heaven and hell issue. Perhaps no one ever took the time to explain to them that yes, indeed, the Bible is true. More and more, science and history are agreeing with the authenticity of the Bible. So, if it is true, then it can be trusted. And the Bible explains that both heaven and hell are actual places. When you believe in your heart that Jesus is the Son of God and that God raised Him from the dead, you will be saved (Romans 10:9). Saved from what? Saved from spending eternity in hell, forever separated from God.

God lives in heaven. When you become part of His family through Jesus, you too will live in heaven when you die.

The teenagers who believed in Jesus and knew that they are going to heaven when they die were much less frightened of death.

More Fears to Come

Once again, the questionnaire showed more stresses over the future than can be addressed individually. So, here's a brief listing of other pertinent worries over the future.

Nuclear war. Will the world end in a gigantic nuclear explosion? Will the superpowers lock horns so tight or thirst for control so desperately that they will resort to nuclear war? Though there is talk of disarmament, is anybody really doing it? These are questions many teens are asking. One suggestion to help calm your fears: search through the Book of Revelation, the last book in the Bible. Can you find any talk of nuclear destruction putting an end to human existence?

The great quake. All the talk and predictions of a major earthquake coming have caused concern among many teens. When will it happen? Where will it happen? Will it really ever happen? Earthquakes, hurricanes, tornadoes—natural disasters, as they are called—are not worth your losing sleep over. If and when they come, the Lord will help us deal with the consequences. Only He can intervene in these instances.

AIDS. AIDS continues to spread at an alarming rate. Not only is it a sexually transmitted disease, but many have contacted the virus through blood transfusions, needles, or birth. Will a cure be found? Will people stop being so sexually promiscuous? Will they turn their hearts and lives to following the Lord's commandments? And what about other incurable diseases? Is there hope for the future?

Children. Many teens wondered if it would be a good idea to have kids of their own down the road. And if so, how many? What if they and their spouses worked full-time? Would their living standards have to be altered to afford children? Are they equipped to raise another human being? Would they be patient enough to have that kind of twenty-four-hour responsibility?

Growing old. Most teens aren't plagued with thoughts of wrinkles, canes, gray hair, and trifocal glasses. But thoughts about growing old do shoot through their brains occasionally. One teen reported that what bothered him most about getting old was not being able to do things he used to do. A young lady shared that it was the idea of possibly getting sick and not being able to take care of herself that stressed her.

Other issues like the economy, the homeless, the job market are also valid fears of the future. How comforting it is to know that whether we're stressed over our career, our success, or nuclear war, the Lord holds it all in His hands. Give your fears of the future over to Him!

Express Yourself

What are your fears of the future? Do you worry about a career, a marriage partner, being a success, death and dying, nuclear war, going to heaven, growing old, others? Identify and record your stresses here.

Your personal fears of the future:

Stress-Relieving Scriptures:

Psalm 34:4 (NAS) — I sought the Lord, and He answered me, and delivered me from all my fears.

2 Timothy 1:7 (KJV) — For God hath not given us the spirit of fear; but of power, and of love, and of a sound mind.

Psalm 32:8 — I will instruct you (says the Lord) and guide you along the best pathway for your life; I will advise you and watch your progress.

Psalm 71:7, 8 — My success—at which so many stand amazed—is because you are my mighty protector. All day long I'll praise and honor you, O God, for all that you have done for me.

Proverbs 3:25, 26 — You need not be afraid of disaster or the plots of wicked men, for the Lord is with you; he protects you.

13 The Rush-Hour Life-Style

Too much to juggle?

Busy, busy, busy. Hurry, hurry, hurry. Go, go, go. That's how the American life-style keeps going. We have become quite a production-oriented society, and that often causes us to judge our personal value by our accomplishments. We are a society that judges its success by the labels it wears and the cars it drives. Our image consciousness itself contributes to our stress.

In fact, our society causes many of our stresses, forcing teens to grow up too fast, pressuring them to act like mini-adults, get jobs, be social, dress the "in" way. Society traps teens by forcing them to grow up, then confuses them by saying, "Hey, what do you think you're doing? You're just a kid."

Double messages, extra confusion, major stress.

Check out the life-styles of a few TV teens. Blair Warner: rich, dressed to kill, in charge, ruled by her appointment book. Alex P. Keaton: suit and tie, money-minded, self-centered, on the go. Vanessa and Theo Huxtable: very cool, very together.

Have you ever seen the Huxtable family all eat a meal at the same time? It seems they all live in the same house, but each one has his or her own schedule, activities, and priorities.

Good or bad, the rush-hour life-style is definitely in fashion. Television and movies glamorize the fast-paced life, and teens are being influenced. Many teens are taking the on ramp and getting into life's traffic jam. A word of warning: Proceed with caution!

Dazzle to Frazzle

"I am so busy. Not only do I have homework, a job, and responsibilities around the house, I am in lots of clubs," says Paula. "Plus, I volunteer at the children's hospital, which I love. I have a hard time saying no because I like being involved and helping others. But I start getting so overwhelmed. Suddenly, one day it all builds up and hits me. I throw up all day and have diarrhea. I get so tired and weak, I have to stay home from school, plus cancel out on my other activities. Sometimes stress gets the best of me."

Paula lives in the fast lane. She has too much to do and too little time to do it in. She is overcommitted. She loves giving of herself but sometimes goes too far.

Candy was in a total tizzy when she ran into a meeting I was conducting. "I'm so sorry I'm late," she apologized. "I was at a voice lesson and forgot to check my appointment book. I can't believe I just forgot. I'm so booked up and stressed. I can't possibly do one more thing."

Though girls tend to be more trapped in the rush-hour life-style as teenagers, guys are just as susceptible.

Nate is a great musician. He's mean on that keyboard, and even writes his own music. He would like to give more time to his music but he works twenty-five hours a week at the grocery store, saving for college. He also serves on the youth council at his church and is busy heading up food drives to help make hot meals for the homeless in his city. On top of this, Nate has a girlfriend who is sweet but possessive. Keeping all his interests up

and meeting the demands of his schedule and his girlfriend gets to be a hassle. Even though Nate enjoys being
active, he often feels trapped, sort of like his schedule
runs him rather than him running his schedule.

Consider the frazzling facts concerning a life that is
rushed and overcommitted. Paula ran into the first one—
sickness. The body can only try to keep up so long, then
it collapses. We often pump ourselves with caffeine all
day to keep going. We eat junk food on the run, not
having time to prepare a nutritious meal. Just so many
laps around the track and the body drops.

Candy hit the second frazzled fact. Being too busy
sometimes makes you look irresponsible. It's quite
ironic. Here you are, volunteer of the year, having so
many meetings, deadlines, projects, places to be, people
to meet. Little by little it starts to happen. You're late to
this; you forget about that. You didn't do the assignment
the way it was requested. You end up letting people
down and looking irresponsible. If you can't learn to say
no to some activities, you'll go on overload and bomb
out.

When you feel like Nate, you will meet the third frazzled fact: Overcommitted = Out of control! Nate's
schedule was so packed, it dictated his life to him. There
was no time for him to let down. When that out-of-
control feeling hits, it can be scary. Here you've said yes
to so much. Now it is chasing you down like a lion about
to pounce.

You start out with good intentions, but end up frazzled. Then you're no good to anyone, not even yourself!
The dazzle of the life-style gets trampled when you get
caught in the rush. The frazzled feeling, of course, is
caused by that same old culprit—stress.

Wanting the Fog to Lift

Tawny said that when she gets overwhelmed she cries uncontrollably. "I just can't do it all. I don't know where or how to start and I end up crying."

The stress of an overcommitted schedule can cause a person to become indecisive. You don't know which way to go or how you're going to get there. It's like being in a heavy fog.

Tawny knows what it's like to be fogged in. She's been there so often that she has had to learn to find her way out. She offers this advice: "Get organized by making a list of everything you have to do. Then number them from most urgent to least urgent. Start with number one. Just getting started is half the battle."

Other Rush-Hour Anxieties

Organize! Having the knack to live a busy and productive life can be enjoyable. Some people love to organize and be in charge of projects and activities. It may, in fact, be their spiritual gift. It doesn't mean it is stress-free, though.

Inadequacy. Some teens end up feeling inadequate because they can't keep up or because they don't produce as much as a friend or sibling. Try not to compare yourself to others. You are you. Just do your best.

Merry-go-round. For some teens life can spin like a merry-go-round. It doesn't seem to have a beginning or an ending. It just keeps going round and round. How do you get off? Several kids reported their desire to get off the merry-go-round, out of the fast lane, and readjust their lives.

Dare to say no. Some teens were stressed over their inability to say no to requests and responsibilities. They keep saying yes because they don't want others to think they are gutless. Others were afraid of hurting someone's feelings if they said no.

Where do I fit in? Some teens ask, "What about me? How can I fit in?" Perhaps they can schedule an appointment with themselves to take some needed time off. A hectic life-style can steal your personal time.

Being on the go, overcommitted, and hurrying to keep up with a demanding schedule is stressful. The rush-hour life-style is especially stressful if it interferes with your personal time and your devotional time. Start each day with God and your pace will be more peaceful.

Express Yourself

What are your stresses related to life-style? An over-committed schedule, being fooled by the glamour, not having enough time for yourself, family, or friends, being afraid to say no to others' requests? Record and identify your stresses here.

Your personal life-style stresses:

Stress-Relieving Scriptures:

1 Thessalonians 4:11   This should be your ambition: to live a quiet life, minding your own business and doing your own work, just as we told you before.

1 Corinthians 14:33 (NAS)   For God is not a God of confusion but of peace. . . .

Psalm 46:10 (KJV)   Be still, and know that I am God. . . .

Psalm 139:3, 16   You chart the path ahead of me, and tell me where to stop and rest. Every moment, you know where I am. . . . You saw me before I was born and scheduled each day of my life before I began to breathe. Every day was recorded in your Book!

14 Being a Christian in a Non-Christian World

Being a Christian in a non-Christian world is like trying to put a square peg into a round hole. It doesn't quite fit. Even if the sharp corner of the square peg were chipped off, the fit would never be perfect.

That is what it is like being a Christian in today's world. You don't quite fit the world's mold; you're just a little out of place. To those of you who have suffered the rejection of not going along with the crowd and may be feeling left out—Congratulations! You are right on track.

Though it's not easy to accept, the Bible teaches that we are not to fit into this world. We are *in* this world, but we are no longer *of* this world after we become Christians. We belong to our heavenly Father's world—the Kingdom of God.

The world belongs to Satan and is very corrupt. Those who don't know Jesus Christ as their Lord and Savior feel perfectly at home here. Those who have Jesus living in their hearts feel homesick, for their real citizenship is in heaven.

When you are a Christian you adopt a new set of values. It's a value system opposite to that of the world. The world's value system says be selfish, live only for yourself, ignore your neighbor, live sinfully. The Christian value system says give to others, live for the Lord, love your neighbor, live pure.

Does having a Christian value system, yet living in the world create tension, conflict, and stress in a teenager's life? Yes! But the amount of stress it causes depends on how closely that teen lives to the Christian value system. It also depends on whether or not the teen is bothered when or if he strays from those values.

Some teenagers felt very stressed-out over being Christian in a non-Christian world; others did not. Yet the issues that frustrated teens the most are common to Christians in general. Let's take a look at some of them.

Staying Straight

Choosing to go against the grain is bound to give you splinters. But chalk up each splinter as a victory for you! "But what about the sting that I feel?" you ask. Well, that's the hard part.

When you don't participate in the lying, cheating, stealing, drinking, drugs, or premarital sex (just to mention the biggies), you often get pressure and persecution from others. Sin is never comfortable by itself. It wants to get everybody mixed up in its evil ways. You may suffer ridicule for your decision to be straight and live a life close to the Lord.

"No one respects my way of life."

"I feel misunderstood."

"I struggle because some of my friends can't accept me as I am."

I won't tell you it's not a lonely path. I've been there myself. Feeling different is not comfortable, especially for teenagers.

"Some kids give in to peer pressure because they don't want to feel left out, not because anyone is forcing them to participate." A wise young lady shared this thought with me. I had not looked at the situation from this viewpoint, yet I know now that it's true. For some teenagers the rejected feelings are much harder to cope with. So they participate for the sake of feeling included.

This is one reason why having Christian friends is so important. There is strength in numbers. But even if you are alone, the Lord is on your side.

Selfish: To Be or Not to Be

What about being selfish? Our world tells us to look out for ourselves, not to be concerned with others. Many successful business people have risen to the top by stepping on and using the people under them.

"Even when I do something for someone, just because I'm being nice, I get teased," reported Roberta. "I really don't like being thought of as a goody-two-shoes, yet I want to help others and think of them before myself. After all, Jesus died so I could learn to love and be giving."

Roberta is struggling with the other kids' reaction to her being unselfish. If it was normal to be unselfish, more people would be that way. But it's not. Our human nature wants to be greedy. But those who know Jesus have a tugging on their hearts to be different. Sure, the other kids may tease, but it's the Lord you will please.

Following through with your decision to serve the Lord can be stressful in today's world. True service takes a heart that is learning to ask the question, "What can I do for you?" instead of, "What can I do for myself?"

Tug-of-War

"Being a leader at my school has been rough," said Darien. "I think I have done well at setting an example for others. But at times, I've hated it because I've also wanted to be part of the gang, so to speak, and to fit in. But that doesn't work too well if you want to be the kind of person others look up to."

Darien is in a tug-of-war. He wants to be a leader at his school—not just a good student, but an active Christian—yet, he wants to hang out like the rest of the kids. He is wise to realize that students who are having a positive influence on others, students who are looked up to, don't fit in just "hanging out." That is the challenge of leadership, especially Christian leadership.

"I feel the other people at school are always watching me," Jackie told me. "It's like they would love to see me screw up, to get in trouble, to get drunk, to cheat on a test, to cut class, to swear—anything wrong. It makes me try even harder not to lower myself to that."

Jackie felt the pressure of having all "eyes on you." It is true, Christians are watched. Sometimes you feel you're on display. Sure, some kids would like to see you fall. But most of them, deep inside, admire you. In fact, it gives them the courage to live straight themselves.

The pull and tug to be less than your best is strong, but let the Lord's hand lift you up above the worldly rubble to new heights.

Tackling Temptations

Jamie is tackling some very trying temptations. "The thing that stresses me is how hard it is sometimes to be a Christian. I have to admit that drinking is tempting," he said. "It looks fun, plus one drink seems harmless. It's so tempting."

Jamie is stressed-out by the temptations he faces. Our society dangles all kinds of temptations in front of us. They are always sugarcoated so you see the fun, not the fire. But watch out, you might get burned.

Being tempted is stressful. It makes you aware of

where you stand on issues. It also makes you aware of
who you are serving, God or Satan. When you defeat the
temptation, you're on solid ground.

James 1:13 explains that temptations are not from God.
God does not tempt His children. The Bible's definition
of temptation means to solicit a person to evil. Webster's
dictionary puts it like this: "to entice, to do wrong by
promise of pleasure or gain."

Isn't that how Satan works? He makes evil look good.
He shows us the pleasure, not the pain. He makes us
promises he can't keep.

Standing your ground, saying no to temptations is
hard. It may mean being home on Friday night, watching
videos with a friend or your family, when half the school
is at a party. Or not cheating on your history exam. Or
telling the truth when you're asked who pulled the
school fire alarm. Or kissing your date good night and
cutting the evening short when you can't seem to control
your urges for passion. Get the picture?

The consequences of giving in to temptation are not
worth the momentary pleasure you think you will have.

"I'm a classic example of someone who was fooled,"
said Krista. "I knew my friends had been messing around
with cocaine. I heard their stories afterwards. They were
wild and sounded sort of fun and adventurous. So when
I was invited to go up 'the hill,' I knew what it meant. I
tried the cocaine. It didn't seem to have much of an effect,
so I had more. I felt so weird, and my nose started to
burn. I have serious sinus problems, but never thought
about that ahead of time. I ended up having to go to the
doctor. My parents found out; it was awful."

Krista's recollection of the night on the hill is not a good
memory. The dusty white powder looked harmless. But
it wasn't. Sure, it was probably exciting and a bit scary at
first, but then the mask was removed. The sugarcoating
was licked off.

Temptations are hard but not impossible to resist. These are tough times. Tough choices. Don't be fooled.

Additional Christian Stresses

Choosing the right path. One girl shared that she gets confused over what is the right thing to do, especially about things the Bible doesn't address. Most teens really want to do what is right. Yet, trying to figure out exactly what that is can be the pits.

Caring about other Christian teens. Some teens feel stressed over other Christian teens. They reported that it worries them when teenagers who say they are Christians do all the things the non-Christian kids do. They felt that showing the world a double standard was no way to win those other teens over to Christ.

Choosing Christian duties. Going to church every Sunday and regular attendance in Sunday school was reported as being stressful. It is especially stressful when you know some of your friends are home in bed fast asleep.

Living in balance. Several teenagers found it difficult to balance their lives between church and school. Yes, they wanted to be in the youth group, assist at children's church, baby-sit in the church nursery, sing in the youth choir, be on the church basketball team, and do all their school activities. Finding a good balance frustrated them.

Being sin conscious. "I feel like everything I do is wrong," reported one student. I've heard this complaint before. To some people the Bible seems like a Book of "Thou shalt nots." Some think the Christian life-style is too restricting. Yet, all of God's "Thou shalt nots" are there to protect us from the sting of sin. Dig a little deeper and you'll find the hidden treasures in obedience. The Christian life is a life of freedom in God.

Living as a Christian in this world of ours is not easy.

A square peg in a round hole. The fit is not right. But don't lose heart. Serving the Lord brings more joy, peace, and contentment than this world can offer.

Express Yourself

What stresses do you have being a Christian in a non-Christian world? Opposing values, staying straight, being unselfish, being tempted, being committed to your commitment to God, going to church, others? Identify and record your stresses here.

Your personal stresses over being a Christian in a non-Christian world:

Stress-Relieving Scriptures:

1 Timothy 4:12 (NAS) Let no one look down on your youthfulness, but rather in speech, conduct, love, faith and purity, show yourself an example of those who believe.

1 John 2:16 For all these worldly things, these evil desires—the craze for sex, the ambition to buy everything that appeals to you, and the pride that comes from wealth and importance—these are not from God. They are from this evil world itself.

James 3:16 For wherever there is jealousy or selfish ambition, there will be disorder and every other kind of evil.

John 16:33 (NAS) These things I have spoken to you, that in Me you may have peace. In the world you have tribulation, but take courage; I have overcome the world.

1 Corinthians 10:13 (NAS) . . . God is faithful, who will not allow you to be tempted beyond what you are able, but with the temptation will provide the way of escape also, that you may be able to endure it.

15 Beyond Normal Stress: Special Situations

The major causes of stress we have discussed so far are school, parents, brothers and sisters, friends, dating, popularity, self-image, money, the future, the rush-hour life-style, and being a Christian. They are stresses we can all relate to more or less.

As the questionnaires came back to me, however, many teens shared unique situations that stressed them more than the average causes of stress.

These stories are true. Like the old detective stories, I have changed some names and scrambled a few facts to protect the identities of the people. To each of these teens I say thank you for being willing to share your story. Each of you is a hero in my eyes for enduring through your tough times and for relying on the Lord for strength and guidance. I hope that you, the reader, will gain an appreciation and sensitivity for those around you who are struggling through the stresses of their special situations.

Wheelchair Bound

Luke was born with spina bifida. This is a disease of the spine which leaves a person stunted in growth and confined to a wheelchair.

Life is hard for Luke. He struggles with the clumsiness of his chair and juggling his schoolbooks. During class changes he steers his way slowly down the halls, trying to avoid a collision with other hustling students. Luke is not able to participate in sports, though he wishes he could.

"Just watching the other guys run, shoot baskets, swim laps, or score a touchdown makes me wish I could leap from this chair," confessed Luke. Luke's social life is a bit frustrating as well. He's never gone to a school dance or on a date. He has friends but only those who are able to cope with his limitations.

What stresses Luke? From the description I just gave I bet you could identify several of his stresses. Being in a wheelchair, needing help from others, not being able to participate in sports or social functions. What about getting dressed, bathing, transportation, the ridicule from the other students? What about the wiseguy who grabs his chair and pushes him fast or tries to "pop a wheelie"? What about his desire for a girlfriend and, someday, a wife and family of his own? What about the stress of wondering how long he will live because of his disease?

Yet, Luke's life is better than that of many kids. Luke has learned to turn to God, and he is learning to be content in his situation. Luke is peaceful and gracious, happy to be alive. He does well in school, has a part-time job, and even has his driver's license. His positive attitude helps to counterbalance the extra stress he deals with every day. From Jesus he gains the strength to continue.

Dealing With Deafness

Annie's face shines brightly every time I see her. Though I don't see her as often as I would like, she always has a kind word to say. Yet, Annie sometimes struggles with understanding people and with being understood. Annie is profoundly deaf.

She speaks with a slightly different sound to her voice.

She has worked hard to learn how to enunciate her
words. Annie sometimes has a problem understanding
because she "reads" the lips of the person talking to her.
She wears hearing aids that allow her to hear to some
extent when she is within close range of the person
talking. If someone is behind her, she may not hear or
may not know where the sound she hears is coming
from. Even though she has hearing aids, she says, she
also misses a lot.

Annie's hearing aids are real friends to her, yet they are
noticeable to others, a hassle to care for, and sometimes
they whistle with "feedback."

What kind of stress does Annie encounter in an average day? Here's what she told me:

> My main stress this year has been the loneliness I have
> experienced. I have longed for a Christian best friend at
> school who is willing to spend time and is mature enough
> to be patient with a deaf person. I know it is harder to be
> friends with a deaf person because it can take extra time.
> Time to repeat a question or conversation to make sure I
> understand. Or maybe they don't want to hassle with the
> "relay services" in order to talk to me on the telephone.
> Deafness really is more of a communication handicap
> than a hearing loss.

Everyone needs a friend, no matter what the situation
is. Annie continues, "I always feel awkward introducing
myself to hearing people, especially my peers and particularly guys. I don't know what they will think of my
voice when I speak or, again, I am afraid that I won't be
able to understand them. I don't want to get hurt if they
think there is something wrong with me. I have desires
to feel accepted. Deaf people have feelings too!"

Annie also has to work harder in school than a hearing
teen. She has needed the assistance of tutor/note taker to
help her get through some classes. All things considered,

she has done remarkably well, earning a 3.6 GPA in a regular high school.

Annie needs to see the teacher's lips when he lectures and also the students who are answering questions. A rush of heat runs up her neck every time the teacher reminds the class to "Look toward Annie when you talk so she can understand you." It's a constant reminder of her deafness.

> I had to quit one job I had a few years ago. I worked in a restaurant as a busgirl and it got too embarrassing when I didn't know people were talking to me or when I misunderstood them. One day a man asked for napkins; I thought he said lemons. He was surprised when I delivered a plate of sliced lemons to his table. I don't like being in situations like that where I end up feeling frustrated and embarrassed.

In spite of all Annie has been through, she remains close to the Lord.

"Many stresses have come because of my deafness, but I thank God a whole bunch for the way He made me. I would *not* trade myself with anyone and I *don't* blame God one bit for my deafness. Everyone has areas of challenge; this just happens to be mine."

Annie has not allowed her stresses to build up bitterness in her heart. In truth, it is her love for the Lord that has been a strength to her.

> When I'm stressed, my relationship with God is a strong bond of friendship because there is no one else to turn to that knows me better than He does. God loves me and understands me. Turning my thoughts to God often can bring peace over me. I have felt more stress this year, but I also felt closer to God than ever before.

Annie has struggled through many stresses in her teen years. Her faith has been a testimony that has touched the hearts of many, whether she is aware of it or not. One of these hearts is mine. Thanks, Annie.

Difficult Dyslexia

Tim was diagnosed with dyslexia in the fifth grade. Until that time he had struggled through school, often feeling dumb because he couldn't learn like the other kids.

Dyslexia is a learning disability that affects reading. There are various complications caused by dyslexia such as the mind reversing numbers or letters. What the eye sees is not what the brain interprets.

In Tim's case he has a visual memory loss causing him to forget what he reads and to see letters and numbers backwards. Tim can remember things when he hears them, but if he reads something he has to read it over and over to remember.

Tim's dyslexia has caused him stress at school.

> Writing and spelling have been the toughest. I spell words the way they sound but that's not always right. The "f" sound might be spelled with a "ph," so spelling is hard for me. It also takes me much longer to do my homework, sometimes hours longer than normal. I have to work harder than the other kids and it's very frustrating. I don't like feeling behind all the time.

For years Tim didn't want other kids to know he was dyslexic. He never showed his report card to anyone and wouldn't discuss his grades.

"I used to feel like I didn't belong with the other kids who were smart. I felt out of place. I didn't want to feel stupid and have them reject me."

Tim's stress over his dyslexia contributed to his lack of confidence. He is the quiet type anyway, and this added to it. He was self-conscious and feared rejection.

In his junior year, Tim began admitting his dyslexia to himself and others. He also tightened his relationship with the Lord and his confidence began to build.

Tim has started to attempt things he never did before. For instance, he has become a dedicated cyclist. He enjoys tackling tough hills because it makes him depend on the Lord for help. It also helps him relieve his stress and feel more at peace.

In the fall Tim will be entering a college especially for dyslexics. The small classes will provide the individual attention he needs to continue his education. This will alleviate some of his school-related stresses and allow him to continue to learn.

Sexual Abuse

Lindsay was ten when she was first sexually molested by her uncle. Then her cousin molested her. For many years she lived with the heavy weight of her secret. She has not developed any serious dating relationships as a teen because of the memories that plague her.

Many of the girls at school bragged about their boyfriends and their "first time." They made it sound so magical. For Lindsay it was a wound she preferred not to reopen. She knew they were exaggerating, yet she wondered if she would ever get over her hurts.

She had become a Christian in junior high. She turned to the Lord to help her through her times of anguish and flashbacks.

For Ashley it was different. Her abuser was her father. Before her mother found out, Ashley feared going home after school and going to bed at night. Now her whole family is in counseling, and, with the help of the pastor, they are working through the situation.

Even for those of us who have not experienced this situation it is easy to imagine the extra stress these girls have been put through. The fear, the self-consciousness, the guilt, the hatred they have felt toward their abusers, have all made their lives tougher.

I pray that each teen who has ever been in this special situation will confide in a Christian counselor and turn his or her hurting heart to the Lord. He is able to comfort you and help you to forgive and to forget.

Foster Care

"I put myself into the foster-care program eight months ago," seventeen-year-old Danielle told me. "I know that sounds crazy, but living at campgrounds was hard. My mom and I didn't have a home, just a camper. We moved from one campsite to another. It got rough. I had a hard time getting to school. Most of the time we were so far away, I couldn't get a ride. It was hard to keep up, but I struggled and managed to get good grades. Foster care was a way I could stay in one place and continue to go to school."

As we continued to talk, Danielle shared the stresses she has encountered. To begin with she has been in three foster homes in eight months. Each set of foster parents has been different; some more likable than others; some more strict than others. Most of them are untrusting, at first.

"Being a foster kid I always feel like I have to prove myself before people will trust me. It's sort of like you're guilty until proven innocent." Danielle told me.

Her case is different from that of most foster kids because she went into it by choice.

After talking to Danielle and several other foster kids, here are some of the stresses they expressed.

Getting around is hard because foster parents are not always willing to provide rides. The kids don't like asking other people for rides, but sometimes they have no choice. Often, you can't get a driver's license until age eighteen, as was Danielle's case. Therefore, she couldn't get a car to provide her own transportation.

Having enough cash on hand is a problem. Like many foster teens, Danielle was forced to get a job. Many times the foster parents don't or aren't advised to give an allowance. Asking them for money is difficult for the teens. They felt embarrassed or resentful.

Most of the foster teens wish they had a "real" family. Many of them come from divorced or abusive homes to which they will never return. They get stressed about wanting the specialness of a close family. One young man said it riled him that neither his real mom nor his foster parents showed up at the school play when he had the lead part. He felt angry and neglected.

Foster kids, like Alicia, seem to experience more loneliness than other kids.

"I personally have never felt part of any of my foster families. When you get transferred around a lot, you don't feel real wanted or part of any family," shared Alicia. "That's the most stressful part of foster care for me."

Being a foster kid magnifies many stresses and creates stresses for the teens who are in this special situation. With today's divorce rate and troubled families, more teens are having to enter foster care. To Danielle, Alicia, and the others like them I say—you are not alone. The Lord walks with you each day. It's comforting to know you have a permanent heavenly Father available to you and that you can be a permanent part of His family. You *are* loved!

Ridicule

To *ridicule* means to make fun of someone or to mock him in a sarcastic way. The average teen deals with the stress of being ridiculed occasionally by friends who are being cruel that day, or by a group of "hot stuff" students. If the typical teen has a hard time dealing with ridicule, imagine what it must be like for those with these special situations.

So many times these teens end up being the brunt of a joke or blamed for doing things they didn't do.

They are also often misunderstood, especially those with a physical handicap or learning disability. If other kids would give them half a chance they would find out that their special situation doesn't mean they are weirdos. Teens in special situations are just like everyone else deep inside. Won't you be one of the people who will give them a chance and help them through their stresses?

Other Situations

Life creates other special situations that we may overlook, but which are very real to the person living the experience.

Have you ever thought that being in the minority is an extra-stressful situation? A person can be part of the minority for many reasons such as color, beliefs, race, personal preferences.

What about serious illness? That's stressful. When a terminal or critical illness strikes one person in the family, it affects the entire family. One teen shared that his dad's cancer was making things tense around the house. Everyone was worried and uptight, often snapping at each other with little cause. Plus they all had to split up the extra duties around the house to keep things running smoothly.

Another young lady shared that her mom's illness forced them to change the family diet. It was hard adjusting to new foods and especially cutting out things she loved like double-stuffed Oreos and nacho chips.

The list goes on. Living with an alcoholic parent, living one week at each parent's house—alternating because of joint custody, having a grandparent or extra people living in your house, the loss of a loved one. Whether permanent or temporary, big or small, there are many special situations that go beyond everyday issues that cause stress. And the Lord cares about them all.

Express Yourself

Are you or someone you know in a special situation? Is it causing you extra stress? Explain your special situation here and the stresses you feel.

Your special-situation stresses:

Stress-Relieving Scriptures:

Psalm 46:1	God is our refuge and strength, a tested help in times of trouble.
Psalm 9:9, 10	All who are oppressed may come to him. He is a refuge for them in their times of trouble. All those who know your mercy, Lord, will count on you for help. For you have never yet forsaken those who trust in you.
Psalm 68:19	What a glorious Lord! He who daily bears our burdens also gives us our salvation.
Isaiah 41:10	Fear not, for I am with you. Do not be dismayed. I am your God. I will strengthen you; I will help you; I will uphold you with my victorious right hand.
Galatians 6:2 (NAS)	Bear one another's burdens, and thus fulfill the law of Christ.

PART III

Hints for Hangin' Tough

16 The Road Back From Stress

"My name is Jeannie and I'm a recovering stressaholic. I haven't had a total stress-out for eight months now. I used to be plagued with worry, anxiety, headaches, mega zits, and a nervous stomach. My behavior had become irrational. I couldn't sleep. I overate. I had a hard time at school and getting along with my friends. I was impatient and felt hopeless."

Jeannie's confession continued.

"But all of that is changing. I am on the road to recovery, because I am aware of what stresses me, and I'm learning to cope. Though my life may never be stress-free, I don't have to let stress have such a hold on me."

Does that mean there is a road back from a life of stress? Yes! And Jeannie is on it. Anyone want to join her?

Jeannie realized two very important things. First, she was indeed stressed-out. She was able to pinpoint the causes of her stress, and that made it possible to attack her stress right where it hurt!

Second, she realized she couldn't go on the way she was. She needed to change. She had to learn to cope. And now she is getting well.

Stress won't go away just because you hang a "Do Not Disturb" sign from your forehead. It's not that easy. However, taking one step at a time, it's not impossible. Like Jeannie, you may need to understand why it is important to learn to cope. When you can cope with the stress around you, it won't be able to get you down. You'll be able to hang tough!

Why Cope?

By now you have come to know the things in your own life that are stressing you out. Now that you are in touch with your stress, what can you do about it?

Finding out what causes stress is easier than coping with stress—not only for teens, but adults too.

Unfortunately, many teens don't realize that they are trying to find a way to relieve their stress. All they know is that they want life to change. They want to get away or to be swept into a world with no problems. However, that place does not exist here on earth.

If people don't learn how to survive their stress, they can end up living strung-out, high-pressure, rush-hour, or depressed lives. And what will the result be? Unhappiness, illness, and breakdown.

Perhaps you know teens who have tried to run from their stress. They escape into a world of fantasy, often destroying themselves with drugs and alcohol. A newspaper recently reported that thousands of teens die every year in drinking- and drug-related accidents. Thousands more commit suicide. Thousands are murdered by other teens and die of so-called natural accidents. And over a million teens are reported missing each year.

If these are the numbers of teens who became statistics, think of the millions of teens who have just *thought* about turning to drugs, alcohol, running away, or ending their lives.

Do we need to learn to cope with stress? The answer to this question is an obvious yes.

Where will your generation be ten years down the road if they don't learn to cope now? Will the next crop of yuppies make it to age forty, or will everyone be stricken with the latest stress-induced disease: Chronic Fatigue Syndrome?

We will continue to be stress targets unless we learn to handle our stress in a positive way. Some people thrive on a fast-track, pressure-pot sort of existence. They are actually addicted to stress. But it's not a healthy addiction. So you see, coping is vital!

Let's Start Coping

I hope you have realized by now that you aren't alone in your fight against stress. We are all struggling. We are just struggling through different things. No one has got it together 100 percent.

So what do you need to be able to cope with your stress? First, how about learning the difference between positive and negative coping?

Second, would a quick course in relaxation come in handy?

Third, how about some hints on problem solving and organization?

Fourth, learn some practical stress-reducing techniques that can help you minimize and control your stress!

Sound good so far? Well, the best is saved for last: God's answer to stress. Yes, God's into stress reduction. He didn't mean for your life to be a stress mess. He designed you to be able to live at peace on the inside even if there is a storm swirling around you!

Let's get started on the road back from stress.

17 Coping and Copping Out

Just as there are positive and negative stresses, there are also positive and negative ways to cope with stress and problems in general. Mitch and Janice both coped with stressful situations. One positively. One negatively.

Mitch is suffering from a heartbreak. His girlfriend broke up with him last Saturday night. He's upset and angry. At home he is talking back to his parents and he even swore at his brother. His mom thought she could smell liquor on his breath, and she was right. Mitch had been drinking most of the week. When she tried to get him to talk about the breakup, Mitch refused. His mom was afraid he was headed for trouble.

Janice was overbooked. In just two days she had three tests to study for, a report to write for biology class, a banner to make for the dance Friday night, and she was scheduled to work at the restaurant both days! Janice looked at all she had facing her and took a deep breath. She decided to make a schedule and organize herself. Seeing it all on paper helped her make priorities.

After she had studied and gotten home from work, she felt tense. So she put on her favorite music and exercised for about twenty minutes. Now she felt better and was ready to face another hour of studying.

Mitch handled his stress in a negative way. He wasn't coping well with the breakup, and he allowed his anger to get the best of him. He reacted by turning to alcohol. His mom was right, he *was* headed for more trouble than just the initial breakup. What could Mitch have done? He could have talked his problem out with someone or gotten some physical exercise to help release his anger. He had other options.

Janice coped with her stress in a positive way. Rather than getting bent out of shape, she stopped and organized herself, thus getting a clear picture of what was ahead. Then she helped herself relax with her breathing, exercise, and music. Janice minimized her stress. Mitch maximized his! The feeling of being stressed didn't disappear immediately for either of them, but Janice got hers under control. Mitch let his get out of control!

The teens who were surveyed had some enlightening thoughts about how to cope with stress in a positive way. Here are a few of their responses:

Keep a positive attitude
Try harder
Get some help from a trusted adult
Listen to music
Turn it over to God
Go do something you enjoy
Forget about it for a while
Read the Bible
Focus on the good
Shop
Fix what's wrong
Don't give up
Pray
Keep a journal
Exercise
Talk to a counselor
Solve one problem at a time
Get more support
Take a walk and think it over
Don't be so hard on yourself
Learn to adapt and flow
Dance

We are going to take a closer look at some positive, constructive, and effective ways to cope with stress in the following chapters. But we can't overlook the negative ways people cope with stress.

Coping Cop-Outs

Mitch and Janice showed us that you can cope with your stress in a positive way or a negative way. For many teens the negative way of escape may seem the easiest. Usually these ways of coping don't make the problem go away; they add more problems and more stress!

Alcohol is one method of escape that can cause more problems than the original stress caused. Alcohol is a drug. It alters your physical coordination and your ability to reason and to make decisions. Some teens use alcohol to escape from their stress. But alcohol has a way of trapping you instead of freeing you. For the kids who use it, this drug only causes more stress and more problems.

Watch what happens in the lives of the teens who turn to alcohol. They fall apart. Their schoolwork and grades drop, they gain bad reputations, they start having problems at home. They get fired from their jobs, their behavior becomes erratic, and they get into trouble. If they drink and drive they run the risk of killing themselves or someone else.

Many high schools now have a Students Against Driving Drunk (SADD) program. This is a good start. But how about going a step further with SAD—Students Against

Drinking. Our local high school has a group called Student Action Team who promote the alcohol-free, drug-free life-style.

So alcohol is not the answer to stress. And most drugs have an effect similar to that of alcohol. Using marijuana, cocaine, speed, or crack to get high will dump you in the end. Drugging your problems won't cure them.

Some teens try to cope by totally removing themselves from the stressful situation, by running away, for instance. But, again, this just brings more stress. Where will they go? Where will they sleep? Do they have enough money to eat? What about transportation? Thousands of teens run away every year. Some of them never return home or are never heard from again.

People dependency is a temporary way to cope. Clinging to someone can be helpful if it's a healthy situation. But some teens depend too heavily on others to make their decisions, guide them, and to blame if things don't go well. Many teenage romances are based on this type of dependency. But when these relationships get sexual, pregnancy can result. Then girls are faced with the responsibility of raising a child or terminating the pregnancy. Unfortunately, some girls choose to abort their babies. They think there is no other way out. But they are wrong. Still, their stress is not taken care of; they have only created more stress for themselves. Turning to others for short-term support is a good way to cope, but if you depend on someone 100 percent, you'll be setting yourself up for a big letdown.

The most extreme reaction to stress is suicide. Yes, it does get rid of a person's stress, but it also gets rid of the person! Most teens who attempt to commit suicide don't really want to die. They just want their lives to change or things to be different. They can get help if they open up to someone who is capable of helping them. I think it must break God's heart every time a suicide occurs. He can help!

Turning away from the Lord in times of stress only disconnects you from a source that has the power to help relieve stress. I know teens often forget God when they get uptight. They blame Him for their problems or wonder how He could really love them if He lets them have so many stresses.

God doesn't promise us an easy life, but He does promise to help us and to carry our burdens if we come to Him and trust Him. You'll never experience God's ability to help and turn your situation around if you turn away from Him.

How did our surveyed teens respond to the question of negative coping techniques? Here are their opinions of dead-end coping techniques:

Keep it in
Ignore it
Stay home and let it get to you
Keep doing what stresses you
Get drunk
Swear
Throw things
Act without thinking
Take it out on others
Binge eat
Freak out
Turn against God
Procrastinate
Deny it
Watch TV and movies for days
Sleep

The next time stress knocks on your door, remember there are positive ways to handle it. Now let's examine some helpful ways to cope. These are practical stress reducers. And what better way to start than with relaxing!

18 Relax!

Relax? Are you kidding? I'm too stressed to relax!

Relax!

Well, if this is what you are thinking, think about this: You are too stressed *not* to relax! You have to relax before stress tightens its grip. You can't afford to stay stressed. When you are relaxed, little things that would normally set you off won't bother you so much. And the big things won't seem so big!

Do you remember the graph back in chapter 1 that resembled *Jaws*'s teeth? That's when we talked about your stress level needing to come back down to its relaxed state. If your stress level stays high, you're forcing your body to operate continually on alert. Remember all the wear and tear that causes on your body, especially on the immune system?

How will you know when you need to relax? Just listen to your body. Are any of those sneaky stress symptoms showing up? Do you have a headache, a nervous stomach, extra blemishes, diarrhea, racing heart, or a cold you can't kick? How about your emotions? Are you feeling worried, irritable, angry, hopeless, or having crying spells? Check out the complete symptom lists in chapter 2, then check up on yourself. Your symptoms will let you know it's time to relax and give yourself a break!

Training yourself to relax when you feel the stress coming will keep you healthier and will better prepare your body and mind to cope. Relaxing helps to refresh you and renew your energy and give you a new perspective on life.

Do Something You Enjoy

There are many different things you can do to help yourself relax. Participating in an activity you enjoy is one of them. Here are some of the things our teens reported as being enjoyable to them. What about you?

Playing tennis	Running with the dog
Going for ice cream	Talking on the telephone
Reading	Playing video games
Playing basketball	Tossing the Frisbee
Lying down	Playing the piano
Taking a walk	Needlepoint
Baking	Listening to soothing music
Going cycling	Watching TV
Going to the park	Shopping
Eating	Going bowling
Working on the computer	Going to the beach

What activities do you enjoy? A good bike ride or baking a batch of chocolate chip cookies might be just what you need. Nick said that going to a field and tossing the football around with a friend was his favorite way to calm down. They could run, tackle, or just catch. It was fun. And Nick relaxed.

Brenda chooses to bake. The stirring, kneading, and mixing motions release her tension. She said she has to concentrate to make the recipe correctly and feels satisfied when it turns out tasty. Brenda also enjoys giving her goodies away to others. It's fun to make someone happy.

In fact, that may be a cure for you. Taking your focus off yourself and putting it on someone else can relieve stress. Go visit a friend, your grandparents, a nursing home, a children's hospital—anywhere you can give of yourself and bring a smile to someone else's face.

Do what you enjoy. Don't get too sophisticated about it. Fly a kite, roll down a hill, or climb a tree. Be a little kid again. Alternate your activities so they don't get monotonous. Choose group or individual activities. Try to identify three activities you enjoy that help you calm down. That way, they'll be on hand when you need them.

Now, what about when time or your situation don't allow you to go play a game of tennis or run your dog around the neighborhood? These are the times you need some techniques that work quickly to get you relaxed and that you can do almost anywhere.

Deep Breathing

Are you aware that when you get stressed, your breathing pattern changes? The stressed-out breath is short and shallow. You are using only your upper chest area to breathe. Rapid breathing and shortness of breath are common characteristics of stress.

Stress-relief breathing is long and deep. You have to do this purposely, of course. It is a bit more exaggerated than normal breathing. Deep breathing tends to quiet your body down. It also increases your oxygen intake, which has a refreshing effect.

Here's how to get a good, deep breath:

1. Stand with correct posture, keeping your shoulders relaxed, your rib cage lifted, and your chin parallel to the floor. (See *Beautifully Created* for complete information on achieving correct posture.) Let your arms hang at your sides, and place your feet about ten inches apart.
2. Inhaling through your nose, take a deep, long breath, concentrating on filling up your chest, rib cage, then abdomen area. You will be filling your lungs with air and expanding your ribs. Hold for a count of three.
3. Now slowly exhale through your mouth. Feel your abdomen, rib cage, and chest return to normal as the air is

released. Repeat at least five times, focusing on your inhaling and exhaling rhythm.

It's as easy as one, two, three. You may want to add some arm movement at first to help you get a deep breath and remind you to inhale and exhale properly. As you breathe in, slowly raise your arms to the sides, shoulder height, then up over your head until they are straight up. Hold. Now as you exhale, slowly bring your arms back down.

Deep breathing can also be done sitting or lying down. If you are lying down, eliminate the arm movement and concentrate on relaxing your whole body. If you ever feel dizzy or light-headed, don't inhale quite as deeply or stop the exercise.

Tighten and Release to Relax

Tightening up your body, one part at a time, then relaxing the tension will assist you in total relaxation. This needs to be done lying down on your bed, couch, or floor. Place your body as straight as you can with your arms at your sides and your face to the ceiling. Close your eyes. Now beginning at your head, tighten and release from your forehead to your toes! Isolate each area so you concentrate on relaxing just that part of your body. To tighten you may have to bend, flex, squeeze, or stretch. Hold each position five seconds and release. Repeat the exercise in extra tense areas.

Head

1. Roll your head slowly from side to side, then up and down.
2. Raise your eyebrows as high as you can, tightening your forehead. Hold, relax.

3. Now, close your eyes tightly as you wrinkle up your nose and cheeks. Hold for five seconds. Relax.
4. Smile big, relax. Blow up your cheeks, release. Open your mouth as wide as you can, release.

Neck and Shoulders

1. Tuck your chin to your chest to tighten and stretch the back of your neck. Hold, release.
2. Lift your shoulders up toward your ears. Hold, release.
3. Now push your shoulders down into the floor. Hold. Then pull them up toward the ceiling. Hold, release.

Arms and Hands

1. Clench your fists tightly, making your forearm and biceps area tight, and stretch. Hold, release.
2. Spread your fingers as wide as possible. Hold, relax.

Abdomen and Buttocks

1. Tighten your abdomen muscles as you press them down toward your lower back. Hold, release.
2. Take a deep breath, filling your lungs and abdomen area. Hold. Feel the stretch on your back muscles. Release.
3. Squeeze your buttocks tightly. Hold, release.

Legs and Feet

1. Concentrate on your upper thighs. Tighten and release.
2. Now your calves. Flex your foot up and tighten the calf muscles. Hold and release.
3. Now point your toes and stretch. Hold, relax.
4. Curl your toes and tighten your feet. Hold, relax.
5. Rotate your ankles several times. Relax.
6. Take several breaths as you are lying there relaxed.

A Quick Massage

A great way to feel refreshed is to treat yourself to a quick massage. You can even do this to yourself!

The best places to massage are your body's stress or pressure points. These are places where tension tends to build up in your body. They are also places thought to be filled with nerve endings.

Begin with your face and scalp. Place your thumbs on your temples (tender area next to your outer eye) and your index and middle fingertips on the center of your forehead. Slowly use small circular motions to massage up into your scalp on your head. Slowly work every inch! Now use your fingertips to massage your cheeks, jaw, chin, and mouth area. Remember, slow and small circular motions.

Now it's your neck's turn. If you have a headache or carry your tension in your neck and the top of your shoulder muscles, this will feel great! Place your thumbs on your collarbone. Now extend your fingers up over your shoulders down your back. Again, using circular motion, begin to massage. This time you can think of it as kneading your muscles much as you would bread dough or clay. Press hard as you knead and concentrate on the area near the spine. Slowly work your way up the back of your neck into your lower scalp. Reposition your thumbs as necessary.

Next in line are your feet. All those tiny muscles get extra tight from the load they carry all day! Sitting, rest your left foot on top of your right knee. Starting with your heel, press and knead from the center of your foot and between each toe. If your arch feels especially tender, spend a little extra time there, massaging gently. Alternate feet.

Your hands have been doing all the work, but now it's their turn. Beginning with the forearm, massage. Now gently pull each finger from the knuckle to fingertips. Alternate hands.

Of course you can massage any other muscles that are tense or aching. Always concentrate on relaxing the muscles as you massage them.

Maybe you can talk a friend or family member into giving you a good back rub. When I was growing up, nightly back rubs were a tradition in my family. It's also fun to get a group of friends, sit in a line, and rub shoulders all at the same time. What a tension-relieving treat!

Whether you choose to relax through an activity you enjoy, deep breathing, tightening and releasing your muscles, or through a quick massage, it is important that you train yourself to relax when you are feeling stressed. That way you can reduce the stress you feel.

19 The Number One Stress Buster— Exercise!

Exercise is the number one way to pop pent-up stress. Remember back in the early part of the book when we asked what to do when your stress gets bottled up? Well, here's the answer: *Exercise!*

In order for your body to move from the stressed state, physical exertion is the key. Relaxation techniques are great when your situation won't allow you to get away to exercise. But when it does, good hard exercise can't be beat. Exercise will help your body return to its normal, relaxed state and refresh you to continue on.

Benefits of a Good Workout

Physical exercise relieves tension in the body. It also helps create a body that is physically fit. Being fit will help you withstand and cope with the stress more effectively. Regular exercise increases your energy level and physical stamina. When you exercise, your body produces hormones that actually make you feel better. Let's call them health hormones. Physical exercise is more than just making yourself think you feel better; a physiological

148

change actually occurs. These health hormones not only rejuvenate your body, but your mind as well!

Physical exertion invigorates the body and sends more oxygen to the brain. The renewed feeling helps you mentally cope better with the demands and pressures of stress. Exercise also improves the quality of your breathing. And we already know that deep breathing is better for stress reduction than taking short, shallow breaths.

Exercise makes that tough decision and pressure situation seem a lot less ferocious. It helps you think more clearly, gives you a new perspective. Some exercises, like walking or biking, can provide quiet time for you to think through your stresses. Others keep you so involved that troubles fade from your mind, giving you a little break, a mini-vacation, a temporary refuge.

Exercise is a way to blow off some steam and have fun at the same time. Plus, you will be doing your body a great service—burning up calories in the process. A well-kept, physically fit body is also a boost to the old self-image. And that, too, reduces stress!

When Should I Exercise?

Exercise whenever you feel stressed. Exercising on a regular basis will help lessen the stress reaction to what's going on in your life. Think of it as *stress prevention*. You don't have to knock yourself out—exercise for short periods of time, say ten minutes. Do this three or four times a week. This is better than exercising for two hours once a week. However, if you are not the type who enjoys a good jog or game of tennis several times a week, at least exercise when stress is on its way or when you are already stressed. It can provide some instant relief.

The time of day you exercise will depend on your schedule. After school, evenings, and weekends are the most logical. Work around your school schedule. Gentle overall stretching, however, can be done any time of day.

Loosen yourself up with a few simple head rolls, then shoulder rolls: forward, then backward. Then shrug your shoulders up toward your ears, relax. Now a few toe touches, knee bends, and twists at your waist to the left and the right. General stretching like this can be done almost anywhere, even in the privacy of the school rest room or maybe the library. At least it's a quiet activity!

Pay attention when you stretch. Stretching your body can help you locate the places you feel tight and tense. This is probably where you are holding your stress. The neck and shoulder area is the most common place for muscle tension. Try to relax this area. Give yourself a little massage.

Touching My Toes Will Relieve My Stress?

Stretching exercises won't top the stress-reducing list all by themselves. Although simple activities, such as getting out and walking your dog, can be enough to make you feel better, just like stretching, they really aren't enough to kick those health hormones into production. It takes movement that is more deliberate and intense. Some great exercises for really forcing that stress right out of your body are jogging, tennis, weight lifting, racquetball, power walking, a good game of football or basketball, jumping rope, aerobic dance, and cycling—whatever gets you huffing and puffing.

Others that are perhaps less strenuous but equally effective for relaxing are walking, skating, hiking, swimming, and stair climbing. Can you think of some more?

Depending on your personality type you may prefer competitive exercises like racquetball or noncompetitive ones like walking. Either is great.

Spend a few minutes warming up before you begin your exercising and cooling down before you stop. For complete instructions on aerobic and nonaerobic exercises see my book *Beautifully Created,* chapter 6, "Total Fitness." There are also tons of good exercise books on the market. If you have any medical problems consult your doctor before beginning an exercise program.

20 Pull It Together . . . Organize

You met Paul, Candy, Nate, and Tawny earlier. They were all stressed-out from living the rush-hour life-style. As Tawny shared with us, one way to cut down on that stressed-out, overwhelming feeling is to *get organized!*

Keeping tabs on when your assignments are due, when tests are scheduled, which days you work, when your bills are due, when practice starts, and so on will reduce stress. You can be on top of your schedule instead of it being on top of you!

Yes, this means you may need an appointment book, notepad, or a pocket-sized organizer. Don't worry, guys, this doesn't mean you have to carry a briefcase just to get your act together. Simply keep your schedule in your car, locker, or pants pocket. You can even write it on your hand or a scrap of paper until you can transfer it onto your list!

Make a List, Check It Twice

Make a list of all that's going on. Then don't forget to keep checking it to be sure you remember everything. You can't expect your brain to do all the work. Use your list to remember important happenings and dates. That's part of the stress-reduction plan. Plus it frees your brain to concentrate on more important things. The less strain on your brain, the less stress to do your best.

Lists are good for time management as well as remembering what's ahead. First, get a calendar. Look at the month ahead of you. Make a list of this month's activities and dates. Your list will be more complete if you write things on your calendar as soon as you find out about them. Now write down the various things you need to do in preparation for each of those activities. How much preparation you need for each activity will help you determine how soon you need to start preparing in order to be ready and relaxed for the activity. If you are responsible for invitations, refreshments, and decorations, allowing yourself one day of prep time won't be enough. Not allowing yourself enough time is one thing that causes stress. So, plan ahead!

Next, evaluate the week ahead of you. Make note of the activities, dates, and times. Schedule the time to prepare for each activity. Make a detailed list of the things you need to do for that specific week. Include items such as people you need to call or go see, assignments, items you need to purchase, and so on.

Now, you are ready to write your daily list. Are you seeing things that need to be done right away? Great! Make your list. Your daily list will keep you on track and give you a sense of direction for the day!

Now That Your List Is Made . . .

Prioritize! This may not be necessary on your monthly list, but is essential for your weekly and daily lists—especially your daily list! Number the tasks from most urgent to least urgent. Most urgent would be things that absolutely have to get done that day. Start the day working on the first task. Then, if the day doesn't go exactly as you expected (and it rarely does), the less urgent items can be transferred to tomorrow's list. Before you go to bed or the first thing the next morning, make a new list.

Should you choose to use an organizer booklet or a pocket calendar, you will find handy places for addresses, important phone numbers, and an attached notepad and pen as well as a calendar. As you experiment you will find the method that works best for you.

By the way, three-by-five-inch cards or stick-on Post-it notes are terrific for leaving yourself notes during the day. You can also keep a pad and pencil next to your bed. When you think of the things you have to do, write them down. You can sleep better knowing you won't forget it tomorrow!

Divide! In evaluating your list, try dividing your tasks according to when they need to be done—morning, afternoon, or evening. If there is no specific time limit, stick to your prioritized list.

Group! Another way of using your time more efficiently would be to group together tasks that can be done at the same time. This is especially timesaving when you have to drive around to complete your tasks. For example, if you pass the office supply store on your way over to Nancy's to work on your history presentation, stop to pick up the markers, tape, and paper you need to make tomorrow's poster for the school dance. This is better than making two separate trips.

Now is when having a weekly list comes in handy. Look ahead to what is coming up and maybe get a few things done ahead of time. All of these ideas will help reduce the stress that can be caused from disorganization or the indecisive feeling caused by the stress itself.

Your Body's Time Clock

What is your body's time clock? When are you most alert and full of energy, ready to tackle the day's tasks? In the morning? afternoon? evening? Except for the tasks that have to be done at a specific time, other tasks will be completed more efficiently when your body and mind are in peak performance.

The tasks before you will also feel less stressful if you attempt them when your time clock says go!

If you aren't sure of your body's time clock, take a week or so to figure it out. Analyze the way you feel in the morning, afternoon, and evening. Take note of your physical energy and mental alertness. What part of the day are you most calm? This may be your most productive time. When you decide what part of the day is your peak, schedule your tasks accordingly.

Go After Your Goals

One way to get organized and give yourself some direction is to set goals. The unknown is always stressful. With set goals, you will have a sense of direction.

Choose goals that are realistic. If your goals are nearly impossible to meet, you will be setting yourself up for failure. Then what? More stress! Set clear, realistic goals you can work toward and do your best to meet.

What areas can you set goals in? Any area! Scholastics, finances, fitness, career direction, school and community involvement, or spiritual goals, just to name a few.

You can set weekly, monthly, or yearly goals—whatever suits you—whatever keeps you striving for that goal. Lisa likes setting short goals. She says that short goals give her a greater chance of success. Plus every time she accomplishes a goal, it's a boost to her self-image.

Larry feels the same way. Short, obtainable goals make him feel better about himself. His increased confidence encourages him to set even greater goals.

Your goals don't have to be complicated. They can be simple, such as being nice to your brother or sister, showing up for class every day, finishing the book you started reading, or keeping your room clean. Well, to some teens these *are* complicated! Just don't think that your goals are irrelevant. If they matter to you, they are important and valid!

Also, set some long-term goals. Ask yourself what you want to be doing in one year, three years, five years, and ten years from now. Write your answers down and save them. You are not writing your future in cement, but you are giving yourself a direction.

Does This Fit?

Be choosy about activities you get involved in or jobs you volunteer for. Now that you have set some goals, ask yourself if this new activity fits in with your goals. Is it a priority for you at this time in your life? Is it consistent with the direction your life is taking or will it divide you? Will it strengthen you or stretch you too thin, leaving you feeling fragmented?

The question isn't so much whether it is a good or bad activity, club, or project—there are lots of good activities out there—but getting too involved or sending yourself off in too many directions just adds to your stress. Plus, stay away from activities you don't really have time for or just plain don't want to do. Beware of others who would intimidate you into saying yes. Guard yourself!

Schedule Yourself In

Though it may sound ridiculous, you will benefit from blocking out time in your daily and weekly schedule for yourself. If you go to school all day, then work from 3:00 to 6:00 P.M., come home and eat dinner, then do homework until 9:00 P.M., you'll get burned out. Choose at least three times a week to do something you enjoy. Give yourself permission to take a break. Be a friend to yourself. Listen to music, take a hot bath, play a sport, write to a friend, ride your bike, paint, go shopping, whatever you enjoy and helps you to relax. Leisure time recharges your energy battery and helps you keep a good outlook on life. It also reduces that stress you may feel. You are special. Treat yourself that way.

Beware of Time Stealers!

There are time stealers lurking everywhere that will throw off your schedule and stress you out because you feel like you can't get anything done. Time stealers are stress dealers. Watch out, they'll try to get you hooked!

Two of the most frequent time stealers for teens are the two T's: television and telephone! An hour or two fly by when that TV is on and your eyes are glued to the tube. And the telephone? Girls are especially drawn to this one. They can spend days chattering to a friend.

Time stealers can be things that you enjoy but end up spending too much time doing. Allie loves to cook, but by the time she picks her recipe, goes to the grocery store, makes the meal, eats, and cleans up, it takes three hours minimum. Then she is uptight because she has to stay up until midnight doing homework.

What things are time stealers for you? See if you can put limits on them.

Above All Else . . . Be Flexible!

Your stress level is directly related to your ability to be flexible and adapt to changes that come your way. The more flexible you are, the less stressed you will feel. Expect unexpected things to creep up—a traffic jam, a late school bus, a run on the library, a friend you haven't seen in years, an extra-long practice—it could be anything.

Getting off schedule is not the end of the world. That's why it's so important not to have yourself overscheduled. If you allow extra time, you won't be bothered by unexpected events. Try not to see these events as interruptions (especially if they are people). See them as challenges.

Being flexible will also be valuable when life doesn't turn out the way you thought it would. You can set future goals but you cannot hold yourself to every one of them because you can't foresee your future.

Proverbs 16:9 (NAS) says, "The mind of man plans his way, but the Lord directs his steps."

It is important that we remain open and flexible to God's leading in our life. We are sure to have stress if we purposely choose to live in opposition to God's Word and His desired life for us. We stress-out if we stay put when He gently nudges us in a new direction. He is worthy to be trusted. He has a good track record; you can depend on Him.

Following the suggestions in this chapter will help you stay organized, which in turn will kick some of that stress right out of your life!

21 Eat to Beat Stress

Did you know the foods you eat can help you beat stress? Think about it. The foods you choose to eat will have a direct effect on how equipped your body will be to fight back when it's faced with stress! Food is fuel to your body and mind. Certain foods are pro-ductive while others are not. Eating foods that are full of nutrients, vitamins, and protein will give you the strength and energy that allow your body and mind to function at their best.

Dale found out the hard way. He had a tough day of tests, a speech, and basketball practice ahead of him. He even had to endure physical education class third period—a unit on folk dance—which he dreaded. In fact, he hated it. He felt like an uncoordinated klutz. At least he didn't feel like that playing basketball! Yet, the fact that he had gotten into a fight with one of his teammates Saturday night didn't make basketball practice sound like fun either.

Anyway, here he was with a stressful day ahead of him. What did Dale eat to get his day started? What fuel did he fill up on? Sugar Cereal. A nice big bowl of cereal high in sugar. Plus, he grabbed a donut at school before his first class. Sure, it satisfied his immediate hunger, but what sort of energy did it provide for his hectic day?

Dale finished his calculus test and felt mentally taxed. He was starting to get butterflies in the stomach as he thought of the speech he had to give next. Even though his mind was sluggish, his adrenaline was high and kept him going. Dale gave his speech, which left him exhausted. It was average, yet he knows he could have done better. He was tired. The sugar high he started his day with had now vanished. He had no energy-packed back-up fuel to rely on. His body was anxious and yet frazzled. He wanted to be home in bed. But no, now it was time to be twinkle toes. P.E. class. Dale was zapped and it wasn't even noon yet!

A junk food diet will leave your tank on empty, adding to your stress! Eating nutritionally will strengthen your body's defenses against stress. Better yet, eating wisely on a regular basis will ensure your body's best condition when stress builds up.

If always eating nutritiously seems impossible or sounds dull, at least do yourself this favor. If you know stressful times are approaching, plan ahead. Eat well before stress, during stress, and right after. Don't let a lack of fine fuel make you have a stronger reaction to stress than normal. Nor should you let your body get sick from the stress your immune system is fighting off. Of course, eating well when stress has already attacked won't help as a form of prevention, since you can't plan ahead. The best favor you can do for your body is to eat to beat stress!

Best Foods for Best Fuel

Eating nutritiously gives you more energy, a shot of strength, and keeps you in a better mood, all of which are handy in tense times.

Deciding which foods to eat is simple. Just think natural. Natural foods are those grown or made from natural products. Ask yourself, "Is this food natural, and is it in its most natural form?" For instance, take an apple. Is it natural? Yes. Is it in its natural form? If it's raw, yes. If it's in unsweetened apple sauce, it still qualifies. If it's in apple pie? No.

How about a cookie. Is it natural? No. Is it made from other natural products? Well, it probably has an egg or two in it, but overall that doesn't count. But this cookie is a blueberry fig bar, you say. Is the blueberry part full of sugar? Is the cookie part made with white flour? Does it contain artificial color, flavor, or preservatives? Gotcha!

Next, a potato. Natural? Yes. Baked potato. No problem. French fries? Ha! Full of greasy oil. Doesn't count! Go for the most natural foods in their most natural form.

Raw fruits and vegetables absolutely qualify as the best stress-fighting foods. If you prefer your veggies cooked, fine. Steam, bake, or microwave them. Just don't fry them in oil or top them with tons of butter, salt, sour cream, or sauces. Fruits and veggies are also good sources of fiber, which is a necessity for stress-free eating.

Keep your eating balanced. Besides all the fruits and vegetables you want, eat from the grain (bread and cereal) group. Have a glass of milk or yogurt or cottage cheese from the dairy group. For protein, eat meat, poultry, or eggs. The meats to choose for healthy eating are poultry or fish. Limit your red meat intake. Choose meats that are lean and low in fat. Trim visible fat off red meats; skin your poultry.

Foods to avoid are items that are processed, like cheese spreads or luncheon meats, and those that are fried, like french fries, chicken nuggets, onion rings, potato chips, and the like. Also, foods that have a long shelf life are packed with preservatives and salt. Beware!

Sugar can't be overlooked. It's an ally to stress. Commercially processed sugar makes you hyper, edgy, and it raises your blood-sugar level quickly then drops it just as fast. You're up, then you're down. Obvious sugar products like candy, cakes, cookies, ice cream, and so on need to be avoided. Be aware of hidden sugars. Read labels. Other terms for sugar products are *sucrose, lactose, fructose, glucose, dextrose,* and of course there are maple syrup, corn syrup, brown sugar, honey, and molasses. They are basically 100 percent sugar. (*See* my book *Beautifully Created* for additional information on nutrition.)

What You Drink Is Also Linked!

Why have a soda when "you could have had a V-8"? Many drinks are nothing more than chemical concoctions—sodas to be specific. Both sodas and powdered drinks are full of chemicals that are neither nutritious nor healthy.

Fruit juices, vegetable juices, low-fat milk, and water are your best bets, with water ranking as number one. Americans today do not drink enough water. Teens especially! Water is essential to the body. The recommended amount is eight glasses per day. Start with four and work your way up.

Try to avoid caffeine drinks such as colas, tea, coffee, and cocoa. Caffeine is a stimulant. It makes some people hyper, nervous, irritable, or unable to sleep. It obviously doesn't mix well with stress.

The old tradition of a cup of warm milk before bed is founded on solid fact. Milk contains an ingredient that acts as a natural relaxer in the body. It may come in handy some sleepless night!

Vitamins for Vitality!

Even if you are eating right, vitamins are extra protection for your body against the wear and tear of stress. One vitamin that is absolutely essential is vitamin C.

Vitamin C is well known for fighting off colds and other sickness. Great! Since stress weakens your immune system, vitamin C will help keep your resistance level up.

A vitamin B complex is great for keeping your central nervous system intact and functioning properly. This is a must if you are stressed.

Vitamin E is thought to be good for helping the body endure fatigue.

Minerals can be stress busters as well. Calcium aids the nervous system as well as overcoming sleeplessness. Iron combats that overtired feeling. And according to the *Vitamin Bible* by Earl Mindell, magnesium is known as an anti-stress mineral and manganese is great for reducing nervous irritability.

What does all this mean? Vitamins are valuable! All of these stress-relief vitamins and minerals can be had by eating a wide variety of fruits, vegetables, nuts, and whole grains—natural foods in their natural form. Eating healthy will help you get all the necessary vitamins and minerals. You may also find it helpful to take a high-potency multivitamin with multi-minerals daily. Ask your doctor or pharmacist to help you select the best one for you.

Eating Disorders and Stress

In chapter 2, when we discussed the basic behavior signs in reaction to stress, you may have noticed that overeating and refusal to eat were both listed. When a person is stressed, worried, out of control, or feeling backed up into a corner, a common reaction is to overeat, as in binge eating or totally pigging out. Or a person may refuse to eat—as in anorexia nervosa or just plain "keep that food out of my face!"

It is well known that both obesity and self-starvation are linked to stress. The stress itself is not the problem.

Whatever is causing the person to feel stressed is the root problem. Choosing to overeat or undereat are ways that people use food to cope. This, however, qualifies to be listed under the negative coping methods in chapter 17.

Abusing your right to eat or not to eat only causes more stress and, in the long run, you are only punishing yourself.

If you are in the habit of feeding yourself when you are upset, worried, bored, tired, or even excited and in need of a reward, or if your pattern is to not eat because you want to spite someone, feel in control of yourself, or drastically lose weight to feel accepted, now is the time to break those patterns. There are many loving and caring counselors who are eager to help you. Getting your stress talked out and figured out will help get your eating back to normal.

22 Go Ahead, Let It Out!

Tell the whole story, laugh hysterically, cry until you nearly flood the place, hug someone, talk nice to yourself. Your stress will be less when you just let it out!

Physical exercise is great for relieving pent-up physical stress, but when it comes to emotional stress, outlets like these are more effective. In fact, they work like a charm. They won't necessarily solve your stress-producing problem, but they will make you feel much better. So, don't hold back, go ahead and let that stress out!

Talk Therapy

Talking about your troubles is a way of getting them outside of you. You feel like you can handle the situation better—maybe it even looks smaller and more tame—now that you have gotten it out in the open and taken another look at it.

Guys, you might choose a hard jog rather than a good talk for your stress reduction; but take a lesson from the girls—they are great at this—talking helps! Find a person you can trust to confide in. Be sure he or she will keep your information confidential. When we need to talk, we don't want a person who will tell us what to do or will tell our problems to someone else. We want someone who will be a good listener.

Seek out people who are older and wiser and strong in the Lord for those really tough problems. They can help you see your way through the mud, and they can pray for you. It's always comforting to know someone is praying for you, especially when you're too uptight to pray for yourself. Your parents may be just the people to turn to. If not, a youth pastor, priest, minister, guidance counselor, teacher, coach, or a friend's parents. Yes, you can talk to your friends. They can be encouraging and supportive. Sometimes, however, an adult can be more insightful.

Building up a supportive network of family and friends will help in times of stress. Whatever you do, don't carry the problem and stress around on your own strength. Jesus told us to share one another's burdens. We can't do that if we don't know what those burdens are. Be open. If you feel that you don't have anyone to talk to, try seeking outside help. A professional counselor, especially a Christian, will have a friendly ear and caring heart and be eager to see you through. You don't have to feel embarrassed or ashamed about going to a counselor. Sometimes there are things in life your parents or others can't understand, but a trained counselor will. Professional input and direction can get you going on the right track.

I know many teens who have been to counselors and are happier today because of it. It may be hard to open up at first, but remember you are doing this for yourself. You are valuable and important, worth investing in! Getting successfully through your tough stress-filled times is your goal. If it means talking with an unbiased, neutral person who is trained in this area, then go for it.

No matter what you feel, you are never completely alone. As a Christian, you have the heavenly Father and Lord Jesus who are always right there ready to listen. In Isaiah 9:6 Jesus is described as a wonderful counselor. Isaiah 28:29 (NAS) says His counsel is wonderful. A wonderful counselor whose counsel is wonderful. Who could ask for anything more? Both the counselor and His counsel are right there when you need to talk. Talking to God is what prayer is all about. Prayer is one of the keys to having a close, open relationship with the Lord. The more you pray, the more comfortable you will be in talking to Him about everything and anything.

The Little Voice With Ruling Power

Okay. You don't want to admit it, but . . . you talk to yourself. No, you're not getting senile. Everybody does it. We constantly have a conversation going on in our minds and it's perfectly normal. It even has an official name. It's called *self-talk*.

Self-talk is very powerful. We have a tendency to believe everything that little voice says. Its message comes in loud and clear. And whether or not it's a positive message depends on you.

You control your self-talk. And what you say to yourself in the privacy of your mind has a huge effect on your attitudes, emotions, beliefs, and stress level! First something happens, then you think about it and talk it over with yourself. Finally, you make up your mind as to what actually happened and what it means. What you say to yourself about the situation or about yourself is the crucial factor in whether or not your stress level goes up or down.

You can create more stress by saying negative things to yourself. You can get yourself all worked up into a frenzy, or you can calm yourself and build your confidence by saying positive things. Here's how it works.

Say you flunked a test. If you tell yourself that you're stupid and you'll never get into a good college, chances are you'll give up on yourself and start settling for less than your best. If you tell yourself it was only one test and you'll do better next time, you will keep trying and not feel like a failure. Just chalk it up as a learning experience.

Or say you auditioned for the school play but didn't get

a part. If your self-talk goes like this, "I never get what I want, I'm rotten in drama anyway," you'll end up feeling defeated, angry, and depressed. But if your self-talk sounds like this, "It's okay, I'll try out for the next play. Anyway, this way I have time to go out for track. I know I'm pretty good at that." The outcome? You will be encouraged to try again and continue to pursue challenges.

Let's try a case of the jitters. You're in the doctor's waiting room, and you know you're going to have to get a tetanus shot because you've stepped on a nail. Negative self-talk: "I hate shots, they hurt. Those needles are so long and the nurse is rough." What happens? You're sweating from head to toe, your stomach hurts, your heart is jumping out of your chest. Try positive self-talk: "Don't worry. The shot is just a little prick and it's over so fast. Besides, it will keep me from getting sick." Which response builds stress?

Negative self-talk leads to negative conclusions that lead to more stress. Positive self-talk leads to a positive conclusion which leads to less stress.

Be nice to yourself. Talk encouragingly and with confidence. Say things that will calm you down, not stir you up. Avoid phrases like I never, I should, I ought, I must, I can't. Let that little voice on the inside say positive things and watch how you reduce your own stress level.

Self-talk can help in other areas besides stress. Your self-talk can keep you from getting angry, keep you up instead of depressed, help you be confident instead of self-doubting and paranoid, and even help you be brave when you're afraid. Actually, positive self-talk can change your attitudes and calm your emotions in nearly every situation in life! Talk positive to yourself!

Loads of Laughter

One of the oldest, most natural and enjoyable remedies for stress is laughter. Laughing makes your tense muscles relax, your defenses drop, and your stress subside. Laughter lightens your heart and helps you look at life a bit less seriously. It makes you feel refreshed and hopeful. Stress can't stay where laughter is alive!

Proverbs 17:22 says that a cheerful heart does good like a medicine. When you're hurting, you can laugh your way back to health and happiness. When you're stressed, you can laugh your way to relaxation.

Singing, like laughter, makes your heart merry! Singing is therapeutic. It lifts your spirits. When your heart is singing, it's hard for your stress to be so stubborn. It has to let go.

So, go ahead, read the funnies, see a comedy, sing at the top of your lungs, tell some jokes—whatever makes you giggle, belly laugh, chuckle, roll on the floor in hysterics, or laugh until you cry.

The Big Bawl

And when you cry, let it be with all you've got. Make it a big bawl, a true cry session, a serious sob, a total washout. Well, you can have a few controlled tears, too, but it might not feel as cleansing as a good hard cry.

Crying is a terrific emotional release. It's like you're forcing all the stress, anger, frustration, and sadness out through those tears. Of course, people cry when they are happy, too. Crying is an inner cleansing. Afterward, you'll feel drained, relaxed, tired—and ready to start again, taking life in bite-sized chunks, one piece at a time.

Now for the big men: I know society says men can't cry, but it's not true. In fact, only a real man is able to show his wide range of emotions. Give yourself permission to cry. If you cry in private no one will know anyway. Just you and God. Jesus even cried. When his friend Lazarus died, there at the grave site, the Bible's shortest verse John 11:35 (NAS), says, "Jesus wept." That's all it says.

Though things in this life make us cry, when we get to heaven, the eternal life, there will be no more tears. Revelation 21:4 says that Jesus will wipe away all our tears. No more sorrow, no more tears. But until then, let the tears roll. They can let out your stress and, if only for a moment, make you feel like a million!

Nothin' Like a Hug to Keep You Hangin'

Hugs feel so good. They make you feel like the person you are hugging or the one hugging you really cares and is sharing your troubles. Hugs are great encouragers. They make you feel better about yourself. Hugs can chase away fear, loneliness, and tension. A good ol' hug also has a way of saying everything is going to be okay. Hugs, like laughter and crying, can bring healing to your heart.

The qualifications to be a hugger are few. All you need are two arms (or only one), a caring heart, and someone to hug. The best part is that hugging can be done anywhere, whenever it's needed. You can hug at school, home, on a train, in a plane, in the library, at the movies, at the market. And you can hug for any reason. Because you made the basketball team or because you didn't. Hugs are so versatile!

If you are not in the habit of hugging, start with a gentle touch on the arm, a pat on the back, or shake of the hand. Ease your way into it. If you are a hugger, be considerate of those who are not in the hugging habit. A burly bear hug may scare them off. Break them in slowly.

A heartfelt hug is just another good way to keep yourself and others hangin' tough through times of stress. Letting out your thoughts, feelings, emotions will keep your stress level on the decline.

23 Pesky Problems

Got a problem? Then you've also got stress! The unfortunate news is that everyone has some sort of problem and most of us will have problems the rest of our lives. Problems aren't always bad. They can be looked upon as challenges. They keep us alive, thinking, and motivated to grow.

But if you have problems piled up on problems—you've got real problems! If you allow your problems to go unresolved, they'll continue to hang around—and so will the stress. Therefore, you must answer this question:

What Will You Do With Your Problem?

There are many ways to answer this. You *do* have choices, though some are better than others. You can ignore it, blame it on someone else, say it's bad luck, or you can do nothing. You can also act impulsively, moving without thinking. Go ahead, tell them off. Slam that door. Slug him in the gut. Write that nasty letter. Of course, you may just cause yourself *more* problems. Your best bet is to solve the problem.

Even if the problem seems too big, too overwhelming, too tough, it's not impossible to solve. Many teens not only feel stressed because of their problem but also stressed because they don't know how to go about solving it. Double stress.

Here is a basic plan for problem solving. Before you begin solving your problem, relax. You've probably already realized that worrying won't affect the outcome of the problem. But creative problem solving will. Remember, problems are like mountains; they can be conquered one step at a time.

Basic Problem-Solving Plan

Step 1: Identify the problem

> Be honest with yourself about exactly what
> the problem is. Collect facts, not
> opinions. Determine if it is the situation
> or your interpretation of it that is causing
> the problem.

Step 2: Describe your options

> Make a list of all your options, both positive
> and negative. Brainstorm and be creative!
> Now cross off those that you know won't work.
> Prioritize the remaining options from the most
> workable to the least.

Step 3: Evaluate your options

> One by one, think through the pros and cons
> of each option. What are the consequences of
> each option? How would that option affect you
> and others involved?

Step 4: Seek wise counsel

> Ask the advice of an older, mature Christian,
> especially when your options look hazy or too
> numerous. Select someone you trust and respect,
> someone who has already lived through the
> teen years. They will generally have some helpful
> insights.

Step 5: Pray

> Now's the time to take the problem to the Lord.
> Offer your situation up to the Lord to see
> what He wants you to do. Quietly wait for
> His answer. Turn to your Bible to see what it
> has to say about your situation. God may respond
> to your options with a green light—go ahead—
> a yellow light—wait, proceed with caution—
> or a red light—stop! You can often sense
> His direction deep inside.

Step 6: Act on God's answer

> Having sought the Lord, select the option
> that best fits His answer—unless of course He
> gives you a completely *new* option!

No problem is too big for God. Neither is any problem too small for God. He is concerned with all the details of your life, especially the areas that stress you! Psalm 138:7, 8 assures us of the Lord's concern.

With David we can confidently say: "Though I am surrounded by troubles, you will bring me safely through them. You will clench your fist against my angry enemies! Your power will save me. The Lord will work out his plans for my life—for your lovingkindness, Lord, continues forever. Don't abandon me—for you made me."

When we put our stressful problems into the Lord's hand and seek to do His will, He is faithful and able to be trusted. Romans 8:28 (NAS) is a verse worth memorizing. You'll often be able to grab hold of this promise throughout your lifetime as a lifesaving device: "And we know that God causes all things to work together for good to those who love God, to those who are called according to His purpose."

Do you love the Lord? Then you can trust Him to work out the problems in your life for good. With your hand in His you can do it. There is no problem you will ever face that you and God together can't handle.

24 Meditation: Think on These Things

When I suggest meditation I am not talking about chanting while cross-legged on a little pillow, balancing on your knees, with your palms upturned and your thumb and middle finger joined to make a tiny circle! I am talking about the kind of meditation the Bible teaches. The word *meditate* simply means to purposely think deeply about something over and over. The issue is not so much *how* to meditate, but on *what* you meditate.

Psalm 1:2 tells us that blessed is the person who delights in the Word of the Lord and meditates on this Word day and night. As Christians, we are instructed to meditate—to think deeply over and over on God's Word. King David, who wrote most of the Book of Psalms, went so far as to pray that what he said and what he thought about (his meditation) would be pleasing to God.

Psalm 19:14 (NAS) reads:

> Let the words of my mouth and the meditation of my heart be acceptable in Thy sight, O Lord, my rock and my Redeemer.

When we meditate on God's Word it is sure to please the Lord and bless us at the same time.

What does this have to do with stress? A lot! You can use Scriptures from the Bible that apply to your situations to help calm you. God's Word offers us many promises. It also gives some wise advice. Meditation on God's Word will give you extra assurance and confidence during times of stress.

For example, let's say you are upset over your parents' telling you what to do and you feel like rebelling. If you meditate on Ephesians 6:1–3 (NAS) you'll know the best way to respond.

> Children, obey your parents in the Lord, for this is right. Honor your father and mother . . . that it may be well with you, and that you may live long on the earth.

Or perhaps you're in a situation where you feel in need of God's protection. Meditating on this promise from the Lord will help ease that stress.

Psalm 34:7 (NAS) reads:

> The angel of the Lord encamps around those who fear [honor and respect] Him, and rescues them.

God promises that His angels will stick by and rescue those who honor Him. That will not only reduce your stress, but motivate you to keep living for the Lord. Amy Grant's popular song *Angels Watching Over Me* suggests that with every step we take, God's angels are watching over us.

Let's say you are uptight over an important decision you have to make. Proverbs 3:5, 6 (NAS) reads:

> Trust in the Lord with all your heart, and do not lean on your own understanding. In all your ways acknowledge Him and He will make your paths straight.

Trust the Lord, put Him first, and He will direct you. Knowing this will drive that stress far away!

Now let's say you are worried about something. Meditating on this promise and then doing it will help.

Philippians 4:6, 7 reads:

> Don't worry about anything; instead, pray about everything; tell God your needs and don't forget to thank him for his answers. If you do this you will experience God's peace, which is far more wonderful than the human mind can understand. His peace will keep your thoughts and your hearts quiet and at rest as you trust in Christ Jesus.

Quiet thoughts and quiet hearts are those that are not plagued with stress. They are stress-free, well, at least close! And that's our goal.

The next time you feel stressed, find a Scripture promise that deals with your stress. Then lie down, take a few deep breaths, and think deeply about it over and over!

To find Scriptures that will help you, you need to be familiar with the Bible. Reading the Bible several times a week would get you going. There are also two handy booklets available at most Christian bookstores, *The Jesus Person Pocket Promise Book* and *Scripture Keys*. Both take specific topics and then list God's promises concerning that subject. They are helpful in finding Scriptures that apply to your situation. Being armed with God's Word will help you battle your stress.

Seeing Is Believing

When you are relaxed, you may be able to think through your stress-causing situation more clearly. You may even gain a new perspective on the situation. Especially if you pray and ask the Lord to give you insight.

You may also benefit from mentally walking yourself through a situation that is stressing you. This is called *visualization*.

For example, if you have a speech to give for class, imagine yourself preparing the speech, then walking up to the front of the class. Pretend you are looking at the other students. Feel them looking at you. Take a few deep breaths as you see yourself relaxing. Pretend Jesus is standing next to you. Now, see yourself delivering your speech with confidence and good eye contact and facial expression. When you are done, return to your seat.

Imagining yourself confidently doing things that you are apprehensive about relieves some of the stress when it's time to actually do them.

In Proverbs 23:7 (NAS) the Bible says that whatever a person thinks about himself in his heart, that's what he is. What you think of yourself, or the way you see yourself through your mind's eye, will affect your stress level. So if you aren't seeing yourself positively or confidently, you may perform accordingly. Take the time to imagine yourself in a positive and confident way.

Visualization is also helpful when you have a busy day scheduled. Maybe even before you get out of bed, quietly see yourself going through the activities of the day. In a relaxed state you can often remember little details that you may have forgotten later in the rush of the day. Before you get up, ask the Lord to be with you throughout the day, to guide you and strengthen you. It's a great way to start your day!

25 Helpful Hints for Hangin' Tough

For fast, temporary relief, here are a bunch of stress-relief remedies that may help you cope with your stress and keep you hangin' in there. Since we are each unique, the same remedy won't work for everyone. So here are some suggestions you can try out to see what works for you.

Alternate Your Alternatives!

There may be times when you experience several stressful happenings at once. Taking time out for a recreational activity may sound inviting but your time may not allow for it. But you can give yourself a break from your normal stress by doing another activity. It may still be something that creates stress, but just alternating your activities is helpful. Perhaps you are studying for an algebra test. Stop for a while and practice reciting the poem you have to give in English class. Switching activities is the next best thing to a real break! You may still be doing something demanding, but if it requires using a different part of your brain and body, it will feel like a relief. This puts balance in your schedule which adds a boost to your energy. So, alternate your alternatives!

Environment Enrichments

Your environment can have a positive effect on your attitude, mood, perspectives, and personal energy. All of these will affect your stress level.

Decorate your personal space: your bedroom, bathroom, school locker, car—any place that is yours—so that it reflects your likes. Choose a color you enjoy, splash it throughout your room. Add a live plant or fresh-cut flowers, a desktop aquarium, or a small pet for added signs of life! If you like frills, decorate in lace and ruffles. If you like sports, hang some athletic-type posters and keep your sports gear where you can see it as a reminder of something that makes you happy. The same applies for anything you enjoy.

Perhaps your personal space needs to be organized and cleaned up. Great. Add some stackable files, a pencil and pen holder, and the like. Make yourself a desk using cement blocks and a sheet of plywood. Keep your clothes off the floor. Most teens feel less stressed when their environment is neat and orderly. If you feel stressed in your room and messiness is the reason, clean it up! Then paint it, decorate it, make it you!

What about noise? Too much, not enough? Noise makes some people stressed. Turning the music down and the TV off may eliminate bothersome noise when you're feeling tense. This, too, will make your environment more livable.

Sweet Sleep

I can assure you that if you live with pressures and demands from school, friends, dating, family, or so on, and you rob yourself of an appropriate amount of sleep, *you will be stressed-out*. You may also be irritable, accident-prone, too tired to be your best self and to produce your best work.

Your body absolutely needs to be on a consistent sleep schedule, getting the same amount of sleep each night. Though sleeping needs vary from person to person, consistency will be your safeguard. On the average, the body requires seven to eight hours of sleep per night. Sleep recharges, renews, heals, and refreshes your body and mind. You will be adding to your stress if you neglect your sleep.

Oversleeping, on the other hand, is often a sign of stress and depression. Sleep can be an escape from problems and responsibilities. An avoidance tactic! Don't let sleep become that for you. You and the Lord can work out your problems.

Many people benefit from mininaps during the day. A twenty-minute relaxation time, just lying down long enough to fall asleep and wake up fresh. Naps can be great. But beware, they can be habit-forming!

Avoid caffeine late in the day as it frequently interrupts sleep patterns. Drink decaffeinated coffee, caffeine-free colas, and herb teas.

Heat Relief!

Heat has a magical way of relaxing tense muscles and calming your body. Next time you are uptight, take a hot bath. Add a few fragrant bath oil beads or lots of bubbles. Okay, you guys may prefer straight water! Try playing a soft instrumental music cassette or lighting a candle and turning off the lights. Put your head back, close your eyes, and let the hot bathwater relax you.

No time for a bath? A hot cloth on your face or forehead will be perfect. This feels extra wonderful if you happen to have a headache. A heating pad will do the trick on tight shoulder muscles.

Now all you need is a cup of hot herb tea. Aah! Heat relief.

The Right to Change

A great stress-release policy to adopt into your life is the right to change your mind when necessary. Things may happen in ways that you don't expect, causing you to reassess the direction in which you were headed. You may discover that something is not what you thought it was and you should steer away from it.

Though it is very important to keep your word and maintain your integrity, there are times when a change of plan is essential, especially when you are in over your head and the stress is getting the best of you. There are few situations that you are locked into 100 percent. Changing doesn't mean you are weak, especially when you are aware of your personal need for stress reduction.

A Change of Scenery

Getting away for a while is a remedy many have practiced for stress relief. A change of scenery can lift your spirits and keep you going. It's a good time to get away to think or remove yourself from a tense, upsetting, or depressing situation. One teen shared that when she's angry with her parents, she gets out of the house for a while and cools off. Then she can come home and logically discuss the situation with her mom and dad.

A change of scenery can also feel like a minivacation— a chance to set aside your stress, to do something different for a while. Make it a healthy change.

Self-Image Stress

Stress subsides when you do something that makes you feel good about yourself. Sort of a self-image booster. What could you do to make you appreciate and like yourself more? It's important for you to see your own value. People with a healthy self-image are known to cope with stress more effectively than those who dislike and disapprove of themselves.

Is there something you want to change? If it's change-able, go ahead. Things like glasses, braces, weight, clothes, hairstyles can be changed. Height, facial features, parents cannot. Be realistic. Change what you can, accept what you can't. God didn't make a mistake when He designed you. To Him, you are handsome, beautiful, and lovable.

Personality changes are also obtainable. Want to be a more interesting person? Develop new interests and hobbies, read the newspaper, find a cause to give yourself to. Above all, stop expecting perfection from yourself. Concentrate on your strong points while you work on your weak ones. Your self-image stress can be reduced!

Practice Makes Perfect

As you learn practical ways to help you cope with your stress, keep them in the forefront of your mind. Every time you feel stress slipping up on you, turn your favorite stress reducer loose on it! This may take some practice. You may not be used to responding with stress-reducing remedies, but practice makes perfect. Make yourself a note and place it where you'll see it daily. Write down the stress-relief activities that work for you. Let it be a reminder of your new ways to react, your own special secret that keeps you coping.

Though your life may never be completely stress-free, there is no need to buckle under to the demands and pressures of life when you now have available practical ways to help keep you hangin' tough!

26 God's Answer to Stress

Does God have an answer to stress? Does He have a secret solution to the uptight, tense times we live in? When asked this on the questionnaire, many teens confessed that when they get stressed-out, they forget about God. They didn't see how He could help. Boy, are they going to be surprised when they read this chapter and see just how concerned God is about stress and how much He can help. God's plan is for your life to be less stressed!

Several of the teens surveyed did turn to the Lord for stress relief. Tessa had this to say: "When I get stressed, I turn my thoughts to Jesus. I know He understands what I am going through, just as if He had been through it Himself. When I read my Bible and talk to God, I find that He gives me peace in my heart."

Seventeen-year-old Rick said, "I realize that God is there for me all the time. Because I am sold out to God, I allow Him to help me get through the stress. God wants to be part of everyone's life. He wants to share in all of their happiness, all of their sadness, and all of their stress times."

These two teens have learned from experience that God does indeed care about your stress and offers a way to cope. To experience this for yourself, try what worked for Tessa, talk your situation over with the Lord in prayer. Then take Rick's advice. Allow the Lord to help you and be sold out to Him. And the outcome? God's peace.

Peace Through Prayer

What is the opposite of stress? It is inner calmness, better known as peace. The Bible clearly shows that God comes to offer us peace in our lives. It is more than just having the world around us quiet down for a while. God's peace is the kind that gives us a sense of confidence and trust. It fills our hearts, assuring us that with God everything will work out.

Jesus says that His peace is not like the world's peace. John 14:27 (NAS) says, "Peace I leave with you; My peace I give to you; not as the world gives, do I give to you. . . ."

The world's idea of peace is having everything in life go smoothly, having no troubles, having complete quiet, and not letting other people ruffle your feathers. Well, sure, if you move to the top of a high mountain or the deserted desert where there is no one around to bother you, it will be peaceful. But God knows that is not very realistic, nor is that what He wants for our lives. He has asked us to be lights in our world, to get involved and show others who Jesus is. God knows our lives will be stressful at times, and so He offers a different kind of peace. Not peace on the outside, but peace on the inside.

Yet, when your parents are fighting, you have to study for four tests, your date just dumped you, you got fired from your job, or your biology teacher just insulted you in front of the whole class, exactly how do you get this peace that fills you with confidence and trust? Glad you asked! You get this peace through prayer.

Philippians 4:6–9 tells us how:

Don't worry about anything; instead, pray about everything; tell God your needs and don't forget to thank him for his answers. If you do this you will experience God's peace, which is far more wonderful than the human mind can understand. His peace will keep your thoughts and your hearts quiet and at rest as you trust in Christ Jesus.

And now, brothers, as I close this letter let me say this one more thing: Fix your thoughts on what is true and good and right. Think about things that are pure and lovely, and dwell on the fine, good things in others. Think about all you can praise God for and be glad about. Keep putting into practice all you learned from me and saw me doing, and the God of peace will be with you.

Let's examine this passage from Philippians bit by bit to get a better understanding of how this works.

Quit Worrying

The first instruction is to stop worrying! Worrying goes hand in hand with stress. So . . . stop! Worry only causes more problems. Matthew 6:27 says that worry won't add a single moment to your life. In fact, worry takes away from your life. People who are worriers develop heart problems and other diseases more often than nonworriers. Peacefulness actually adds to your life. Proverbs 14:30 (TLB) says that a relaxed attitude lengthens a person's life. Another version agrees, saying a tranquil or peaceful heart adds life to the body. Worry takes away life; peace adds life. So, for your own good, stop worrying!

Pray About Everything

Instead of worrying, we are to pray about everything. Tell all your needs to God. He wants you to talk to Him about every trouble, every problem, every worry, every stress. He is interested in every detail of your life. Don't hold back; let Him have it all!

Whenever possible, choose a place for prayer that is quiet. When there's lots of distraction, we can forget what we're trying to say. The Bible says Jesus usually went to the mountains to be alone and pray. It was quiet and He could openly pour out his heart to His Father God. Well, we don't have to go to the mountains. The idea is to find a quiet place. Matthew 6:6 says to go away by yourself and close the door. Then with openness, honesty, and boldness pray to the Lord. Of course, we can't always have it completely quiet. Many times during the hustle and business of the day we need to shoot those "quickie" prayers up to God. Yet, for your longer prayer times, quiet and solitude are helpful.

Date	Prayer Request	Prayer Answer	Date
	1.		
	2.		
	3.		

Keep a prayer journal handy. Use a booklet with blank pages or a spiral notebook. Write down the date, your prayer request, then leave a column to write in the answer and the date the answer was given. It helps to look back and see how God has worked. It also reminds you that God does, indeed, answer prayer.

Thanks a Lot, God

Our next instruction is to thank God for His answers, even before they come. After you have told God your needs, right away start thanking Him for the solutions and answers! Why thank God before He has done anything? Two reasons. First, thanking Him ahead of time shows Him you have faith that He will indeed give you an answer. Second, it makes you expect an answer! Many kids say a little prayer, walk away, and forget they even prayed at all. Later, they can't remember if God ever did anything. Our part is to pray. God's part is to answer. So thank Him right away and expectantly wait for Him to respond.

The Great Exchange

If you stop worrying, pray about everything, tell God your needs, and thank Him for His answer, what do you get? God's peace! God exchanges your prayer needs, your stresses, for His peace. What a deal!

Better yet, it is a peace that is so wonderful your mind can't understand it. Here you have all these troubles and you should be completely stressed-out, but you're not. You're peaceful. Calm. Confident. You're amazed at your response and so are others.

God's peace has a way of keeping your heart and mind quiet and restful. When you entrust your needs to Jesus, His peace will be yours.

Fix Your Thoughts

Now that you have prayed and God's peace is coming into your heart, what should your thoughts be? Should you wonder if He'll really help you or if He really heard you? Should you start worrying again? No. Turn your thoughts to positive things!

The next instruction is to fix (that's like to glue) your thoughts on things that are true, good, right, pure, and lovely. Think about the fine and good things in others. Plus, think of all the things you can be glad about and praise God for. Keep your thoughts away from evil, fear, doubt, or worry. Think on good things. Think about the Lord.

Isaiah 26:3 promises us that He will keep in perfect peace all those who trust in Him, whose thoughts turn often to the Lord.

Trust the Lord, fixing your thoughts on Him, and you will have peace.

Keep on Practicing

The last instruction in this passage is to keep practicing all these things you have just learned. Don't forget about them. Keep your prayer journal and Bible in a handy place. Set aside a special time each day to pray and be with the Lord. Practice makes perfect, as they say. And practicing your prayer, making it a regular part of your day, will be a guarantee that God's peace will be with you!

Prayer Problems

Many surveyed teens felt that God didn't answer their prayers. They felt their conversations were one-sided. As I mentioned earlier, part of the problem is taken care of when you keep track of your prayers. That helps you remember what you prayed so you can recognize it when God answers.

The problem isn't that God doesn't answer. It's that too often we don't hear His answer or recognize His solution. Here are a few ways to hear from God. Be aware of them and expect His answers.

1. *The Bible.* Many times the answer or encouragement you need is right in the Bible. As you read, a certain Scripture may suddenly have new meaning. It comes alive. It's just what you needed. That's God.

2. *Other People.* Often God will speak to you through something someone says. It catches your attention and applies to your situation. The person may have no idea he said something that helped you. But when someone shares from wisdom and experience, God uses it as an answer.

3. *Inner Listening.* After you pray, sit quietly and listen for the Lord to speak to you. This won't be an audible voice, but in the form of a thought in your mind, one that you know you didn't think up. If it's positive, good, loving,

and in line with the Bible and God's nature, you can trust it. If it's evil or revengeful, it's not God.

4. *Change of Circumstances.* When something that was going wrong suddenly starts working out, or a new option is presented, some call it a coincidence. Well, if it's something you've prayed about, I would call that God. He makes things happen that change our circumstances and answer our prayers.

5. *Follow After Peace.* Another way God can give you direction and answers is through His peace. In the Amplified Bible, Colossians 3:15 says to let God's peace be the umpire in your life. An umpire is the one who calls the shots and makes the final decisions. When you need an answer to a problem, see which direction you feel peaceful going in. God leads through His peace.

Be on the lookout for the Lord, read your Bible, talk with other Christians, follow after peace, and listen for the Holy Spirit to speak. God *does* answer prayer. He does not pick and choose whose prayers He will answer. He answers all prayers in the way He sees fit. Trust His wisdom. He loves you. He will answer.

Sold Out to God

Another way to bring peace into your life, as a Christian, is to be sold out to God. To be committed to serving Him and living your life for Him.

Many teens find this difficult to understand. Yet it's simple. If you are divided on which direction to go with your life, you won't be able to make decisions. You will constantly go back and forth and, consequently, end up going nowhere. Life will be stressful if you, as a Christian, try to live with one foot in the world and one foot in the Kingdom of God. You're going to get hurt trying to straddle the fence! It just doesn't work. You will be pulled from both directions. You'll have no peace.

One teen shared that she felt as if she was on a teeter-totter. She was constantly going up and down—toward God then away from Him. She was being pulled.

The Book of James addresses this problem. James 1:8 says that if you are double-minded you will be unstable in everything you do. Double-minded means to have two minds, two desires, two viewpoints, two beliefs, one foot in the Kingdom, one foot in the world. Wanting to serve God, but wanting to hold hands with the values of this world. When you are divided against yourself, there will be confusion, strife, arguing, and stress! All of these are the opposite of peace.

James 4:8 advises people who are double-minded to draw near to God and to purify their hearts. Get off the teeter-totter, stop straddling the fence. Plant both of your feet in the Kingdom of God and His peace will rule in your heart.

Partnership With God

When you have asked Jesus Christ into your heart to be your Lord and Savior, you enter into partnership with God. You are not living your life alone. Hand in hand God walks with you through the tough times. And during the times of crisis, He carries you. You can rest assured that whether it's through the valley, or on the mountaintop, you are always with the Lord.

God will never leave you or turn away from you. He won't give up on you. You are in this life together, through thick and thin. With God, it is possible to hang tough. You don't have to quit, turn to drugs or alcohol, run away, or think of ending your life. With all the peace and guidance Jesus is ready to give to you, no matter how stressed-out you are, you can keep hangin' tough.

Additional Peace-Producing Scriptures

Ephesians 2:14
(NAS)

For He Himself is our peace. . . .

Matthew 5:9

Happy are those who strive for peace—they shall be called the sons of God.

Proverbs 1:33 (NIV)

But whoever listens to me will live in safety and be at ease, without fear of harm.

Matthew 6:31, 33
(NAS)

Do not be anxious then, saying, shall we eat?" or "What shall we drink?" or "With what shall we clothe ourselves?". . . But seek first His kingdom and His righteousness; and all these things shall be added to you.

Matthew 11:28
(NAS)

Come to Me, all who are weary and heavy-laden, and I will give you rest.

Psalm 34:14

Turn from all known sin and spend your time in doing good. Try to live in peace with everyone; work hard at it.

Psalm 50:15 (NAS)

And call upon Me in the day of trouble; I shall rescue you, and you will honor Me.

Isaiah 40:31 (NAS)

Yet those who wait for the Lord will gain new strength; they will mount up with wings like eagles, they will run and not get tired, they will walk and not become weary.

Dear Friend,

Do you have stress in your life? Are you applying the ideas in this book to help you cope? Are you still puzzled about stress or how to cope with your situation? Feel free to write to me. Let's see if we can work through your stress together. Here's my address:

Andrea Stephens
c/o Beautifully Created
P.O. Box 1405
Santa Ynez, CA 93460